More Tales From Shakespeare

CHARLES AND MARY LAMB

Level 5

Retold by G. Horsley
Series Editors: Andy Hopkins and Jocelyn Potter

Pearson Education Limited
Edinburgh Gate, Harlow,
Essex CM20 2JE, England
and Associated Companies throughout the world.

ISBN 0 582 41934 4

First published in the Longman Simplified English Series 1956
First published in the Longman Fiction Series 1993
This adaptation first published 1996
Third impression 1997
This edition first published 1999

NEW EDITION

This edition copyright © Penguin Books Ltd 1999
Cover design by Bender Richardson White

Set in 11/14pt Bembo
Printed in Spain by Mateu Cromo, S.A.Pinto (Madrid)

Published by Pearson Education Limited in association with
Penguin Books Ltd, both companies being subsidiaries of Pearson Plc

For a complete list of the titles available in the Penguin Readers series please write to your local
Pearson Education office or to: Marketing Department, Penguin Longman Publishing,
5 Bentinck Street, London W1M 5RN.

Contents

Introduction

In 1807 Charles Lamb and his sister Mary Lamb were asked by their good friend, William Godwin, to write the stories from the best-known of Shakespeare's plays in a form that children could easily understand. The stories were intended as an introduction to Shakespeare for readers who were too young to read the plays themselves, and not as a replacement. It was suggested that girls in particular, who would not in those days be able to use libraries as freely as their brothers, would profit from them. The result was *Tales from Shakespeare*. 'I think it will be popular among the little people,' Charles wrote to a friend at the time. And he was right: the stories succeeded beyond expectation, enjoying popularity (with people of all sizes!) until the present day.

At the beginning of the nineteenth century the moral tale was an important form of literature for children; stories were used mainly to teach children the difference between right and wrong. This affected the way the Lambs wrote the stories: the characters are shown as either good or bad in a way that is not so obvious in the plays, and the moral at the end of each story is very clear. The *Tales* attempt, wherever possible, to use Shakespeare's own words to retell the stories, but the language is made easier for the young reader. Some of the stories have also been made less complicated, with fewer characters than the original.

For the Lambs, whose lives until this point had not been at all easy, the *Tales* were their first success in the world of literature. Charles was born in 1775, nine years after Mary Ann. Their father was a poorly paid lawyer's clerk in London. Charles was sent to the well-known Christ's Hospital School, but Mary, as a girl, did not have the opportunity for such a good education as her brother. For most of his life, Charles worked as a clerk at East India House, while writing in his free time. His work was not well paid, and even though Mary earned a little money from needlework, the family was poor. Mary gradually became mentally unbalanced, and then a terrible event took place that changed the brother's and sister's lives for ever. In 1796 their mother tried to stop a fight between Mary and another girl. The fight ended when Mary killed her mother with a knife. At the court case that followed, Mary was judged to be mentally ill and was sent to a mental home. But Charles managed to persuade the courts to let him take responsibility for looking after her, and she was allowed to return home after three years. Charles spent the rest of his life caring for her, and never married. Because she was known to have murdered her mother and to have been in a mental home, the pair had to move house several times. But on the whole they led a calm and happy life together and brought up a child called Emma Isola, who had no parents, as their daughter. Charles died in 1834 and Mary 13 years later.

Charles was a friend of many famous figures of his time, such as the poets Wordsworth and Coleridge. He was a respected and original judge of literature who also wrote poems, plays and stories. With Mary, he wrote several books for children: they retold the story of the *Odyssey* in *The Adventures of Ulysses* (1808); *Mrs Leicester's School* (1809) and *Poetry for Children* (1809) followed.

William Shakespeare, whose plays are retold here in story form, is famous around the world for both his poems and his plays, but very few solid facts are known about his life. He was born in 1564 in Stratford-upon-Avon, England, to the trader John Shakespeare and his wife Mary Arden. He probably went to Stratford Grammar School, which offered free education to local boys. In 1582 he married Anne Hathaway, and they had three children, Susanna, Hamnet and Judith. In 1592 Shakespeare was known to be in London, acting and writing plays, but he may have worked as a schoolmaster before this. Shakespeare became an important member of a theatre company, which performed at two London theatres, the Globe and the Blackfriars. His plays were given special performances at the courts of Queen Elizabeth I and King James I and his success made him a wealthy man. We know that he bought New Place, a large and impressive house in Stratford, for his family. He rebuilt the house, moved his wife and daughters there (his son had died in 1596), and spent his later years there himself when he left London. Shakespeare died in 1616 and was buried in the church in Stratford.

The stories in this collection are taken from plays written at different times in Shakespeare's professional life. *The Taming of the Shrew* is a comedy of character, and one of the first plays that Shakespeare wrote. *The Winter's Tale* was almost his last play. It is called a comedy because the ending is happy, but the characters go through much pain and sorrow before that ending is reached. These two stories were written by Mary Lamb. The other stories were written by Charles, and are examples of Shakespeare's finest tragedies. *Romeo and Juliet* is an early play showing how the joys of young love are destroyed by the hatred of others. *Hamlet*, a terrible tale of revenge, is probably Shakespeare's most famous play. It is jealousy that leads to tragedy in *Othello*, while *King Lear* shows the shocking effects of an old man's bad judgement. This book introduces the reader to some of the most famous characters from Shakespeare's most powerful plays.

The Winter's Tale

CHARACTERS
Leontes, King of Sicily
Mamillius, Prince of Sicily
Camillo
Antigonus
Cleomenes   } lords of Sicily
Dion
Polixenes, King of Bohemia and friend of Leontes
Florizel, a prince, son of Polixenes
An old shepherd, believed to be father of Perdita
Hermione, wife of Leontes, Queen of Sicily
Perdita, daughter of Leontes and Hermione
Paulina, wife of Antigonus
Emilia, a lady serving Hermione

Leontes, King of Sicily, and his queen, the lovely Hermione, once lived together in the greatest happiness. The love that they felt for each other made Leontes so happy that he had nothing left to wish for, except that he sometimes desired to see again his old companion and schoolfriend, Polixenes, King of Bohemia, and to introduce his friend to his queen.

Leontes and Polixenes had been brought up together as children, but after the deaths of their fathers, each one had to rule his own kingdom. So they had not met for many years, though they often exchanged gifts, letters and loving messages.

At last, after repeated invitations, Polixenes came from Bohemia to the Sicilian court to pay his friend Leontes a visit. At first this visit gave nothing but pleasure to Leontes. He begged the queen to show special care and attention to his dear friend and he seemed to have found perfect happiness now that he was with his old companion. They talked about old times; they remembered their schooldays and their youthful games. They told stories of these to Hermione, who always took a cheerful part in these conversations.

When, after a long stay, Polixenes was preparing to leave, Hermione, at her husband's wish, begged him to make his visit longer.

And now this good queen's sorrow began. Polixenes had refused to stay when Leontes asked him, but Hermione's gentle words persuaded him to do so. Leontes had no reason at all to doubt either the honesty of his friend Polixenes or the excellent character of his good queen, but he was immediately seized with an uncontrollable jealousy. Everything that Hermione did for Polixenes, although it was only done to please her husband, increased the unfortunate king's jealousy. Suddenly, Leontes changed from a true friend, and the best and most loving of husbands, into a wild and cruel creature. He sent for Camillo, one of the lords of his court, and told him of his suspicions about his wife's unfaithfulness. Then he ordered Camillo to poison Polixenes.

Camillo was a good man, who knew that there was no truth in Leontes' suspicions. So, instead of poisoning Polixenes, he told him about his master's orders and agreed to escape with him from Sicily. Polixenes, with Camillo's help, arrived safely in his own kingdom of Bohemia. From that time, Camillo lived in the king's court and became his chief friend and adviser.

The escape of Polixenes made the jealous Leontes even more angry. He went to the queen's rooms, where her little son Mamillius was just beginning to tell his mother one of his best stories to amuse her. Taking the child away, the king sent Hermione to prison.

Though Mamillius was only a very young child, he loved his mother dearly. When he saw her treated so badly and realized that she had been taken away from him, he became very unhappy. Gradually he lost his desire to eat and sleep, until it was thought that his sadness would kill him.

When the king had sent his queen to prison, he commanded Cleomenes and Dion, two Sicilian lords, to go to Delphos and ask the oracle at the temple of Apollo if his queen *had* been unfaithful to him.

◆

After Hermione had been in prison for a short time, she gave birth to a daughter. The poor lady was comforted by the sight of her pretty baby, and she said to it: 'My poor little prisoner, I have done as little wrong as you have.'

Hermione had a kind friend, Paulina, who was the wife of Antigonus, another Sicilian lord. When Paulina heard that the queen had given birth to a child, she went to the prison where Hermione was kept and said to Emilia, a lady who served Hermione, 'I pray you, Emilia, tell the good queen that if she will trust me with her baby, I will carry it to the king, its father. His heart may soften when he sees his little child.'

'My lady,' replied Emilia, 'I will tell the queen of your offer. She was wishing today that she had a friend who would dare to show the child to the king.'

'And tell her,' said Paulina, 'that I will speak to Leontes in her defence.'

'May God reward you,' said Emilia, 'for your kindness to our gentle queen!'

Emilia then went to Hermione, who joyfully gave her baby into Paulina's care.

Paulina took the child and forced her way into the presence of the king, although her husband, Antigonus, who feared the king's anger, tried to prevent her. She laid the baby at its father's feet, and made a noble speech to the king in defence of Hermione. She criticized him for his cruelty and begged him to have pity on his wife and child, who had done no wrong. But Paulina's words only increased Leontes' anger, and he ordered Antigonus to take her away.

When Paulina went away, she left the little baby at its father's feet. She thought that when he was alone with it, he would look at it and feel pity for it.

The good Paulina was wrong. As soon as she left, the cruel father ordered Antigonus to take the child out to sea and leave it on some empty shore to die.

Antigonus was not like the good Camillo; he obeyed the orders of Leontes too well. He immediately carried the child on board a ship and sailed out to sea, intending to leave it on the first lonely shore that he could find.

The king was so sure that Hermione was guilty that he did not wait for the return of Cleomenes and Dion from Delphos. While the queen was still weak and miserable at losing her much loved baby, she was brought before all the lords and nobles of his court for a public trial. When that unhappy lady was standing in front of them as a prisoner to receive their judgement, Cleomenes and Dion entered. They told the King that they had the oracle's answer.

Leontes commanded that the words of the oracle should be read aloud, and these were the words:

'Hermione is not guilty, Polixenes blameless, Camillo a true servant, Leontes a jealous and cruel king, and Leontes shall live without an heir unless that which was lost is found.'

The king refused to believe the words of the oracle. He said that the message was a lie invented by the queen's friends, and he asked the judge to continue with the case against the queen. But while he was speaking, a man entered and told him that Prince

Mamillius had died of grief and shame, hearing that his mother was being tried for her life.

When Hermione heard about the death of this dear, loving child who had lost his life because of his grief at her misfortune, she fainted. Leontes himself was made miserable by the news and began to feel pity for his unhappy queen. He ordered Paulina to take her away and help her. Paulina soon returned and told the king that Hermione was dead.

When Leontes heard that the queen was dead, he felt deeply sorry for all his cruelty to her. Now that he thought his treatment of her had broken Hermione's heart, he no longer believed that she was guilty. He also thought that the words of the oracle were true. He realized that 'unless that which was lost is found' (which he believed to be his young daughter), he would be without an heir, now that the young Prince Mamillius was dead. He was prepared to give his kingdom to get his lost daughter back. With such sad thoughts as these, Leontes passed many years in grief and sorrow.

◆

The ship in which Antigonus had carried the baby princess out to sea was driven by a storm on to the coast of Bohemia, the kingdom of the good King Polixenes. Here Antigonus landed, and here he left the little baby.

Antigonus never returned to Sicily to tell Leontes where he had left his daughter, because as he was going back to the ship, a bear came out of the woods and tore him to pieces.

The baby was dressed in rich clothes and jewels, since Hermione had made her look very fine when she sent her to Leontes. Antigonus had tied a piece of paper to her coat, on which he had written the name "Perdita" and words which indirectly suggested her noble birth and misfortune.

The poor baby was found by a shepherd. He was a kind man,

and he carried little Perdita home to his wife, who nursed her lovingly. But the shepherd was poor and so, in order to hide the rich prize which he had found, he left that part of the country. Then, with some of Perdita's jewels, he bought large numbers of sheep and became wealthy. He brought up Perdita as his own child, and she did not know that she was not in fact a shepherd's daughter.

Little Perdita grew up to be a lovely girl. She had no better education than that of a shepherd's daughter, but the noble qualities she had got from her royal mother shone through so clearly that no one would have known she had not been brought up in King Leontes' court.

◆

Polixenes had an only son whose name was Florizel. One day, as this young prince was hunting near the shepherd's home, he saw the girl who was said to be the old man's daughter, and her beauty and noble manner made him fall in love with her immediately. Soon, under the name of Doricles, and dressed as a private gentleman, he became a frequent visitor to the old shepherd's house. Florizel's absences from court made Polixenes anxious, so he ordered people to watch his son and he soon discovered Florizel's love for the shepherd's fair daughter.

Polixenes then sent for Camillo, the same faithful Camillo who had kept him safe from the anger of Leontes, and asked him to go with him to the shepherd's house.

Both Polixenes and Camillo changed their appearances so that they would not be recognized, and arrived at the shepherd's house just as a feast was taking place. Though they were strangers, every guest was made welcome at such a time and they were invited to walk in and join the celebrations. Everyone was happy and joyful. Tables were full of things to eat and drink, and young men and girls were dancing on the grass in front of the house.

Florizel and Perdita were sitting quietly together in a corner, seeming more pleased with each other's conversation than with the games and amusements of those around them.

The king, knowing that he could not be recognized, went near enough to hear their conversation, and was surprised by the simple but graceful manner in which Perdita talked to his son.

'This is the prettiest lowborn girl I have ever seen,' he said to Camillo. 'Everything she does or says seems too noble for this place.'

Then the king turned to the old shepherd and said, 'Tell me, my good friend, who is that young man talking with your daughter?'

'They call him Doricles,' replied the shepherd. 'He says he loves my daughter; and, to tell the truth, it is difficult to know which loves the other best. If young Doricles can win her, she will bring him what he does not dream of.' By this he meant the rest of Perdita's jewels, which he had carefully saved to give her on her wedding day.

Polixenes then spoke to his son. 'Young man,' he said, 'your heart seems full of something that takes your mind away from feasting. When I was young, I used to bring presents for my love, but you seem to have brought nothing for your girl.'

The young prince, who did not know that he was talking to his father, replied, 'Sir, she does not value such things. The gifts which Perdita expects from me are locked up in my heart.'

Then Florizel turned to Perdita and said, 'O hear me, Perdita, before this ancient gentleman who, it seems, was once himself a lover.'

Florizel then called on the stranger to be a witness to a promise of marriage which he made to Perdita, but at that point, the king made himself known to his son and criticized him for daring to promise to marry this lowborn girl. He called Perdita disrespectful names, and threatened that if she ever allowed his son to see her again, he would put her and the old shepherd to a cruel death.

The king left them then in great anger, and ordered Camillo to follow him with Prince Florizel.

When the king had gone, Perdita, whose royal nature was excited by Polixenes' angry words, said, 'Though our hopes are now destroyed, I was not much afraid. Once or twice I was going to speak, and to remind him that the same sun that shines on his palace also shines on our small house.'

Then she added sadly, 'But now I am woken from this dream. Leave me, sir; I will go to my sheep and cry there.'

The kind-hearted Camillo was greatly affected by Perdita's behaviour. He saw that the young prince was too deeply in love with her to give her up at the command of his royal father. So he thought of a way to help them both and, at the same time, to put into action a plan which he had in his mind.

Camillo had known for a long time that Leontes, the King of Sicily, was truly sorry for all he had done; and though Camillo was now the favourite adviser of King Polixenes, he could not help wishing to see his old master and his home once more. He therefore suggested to Florizel and Perdita that they should go with him to the Sicilian court, where he promised that Leontes would protect them. Then, with his help, they could obtain forgiveness from Polixenes and his agreement to their marriage.

They joyfully agreed to this plan, and Camillo also allowed the old shepherd to go with them.

The shepherd took with him the rest of Perdita's jewels, her baby clothes, and the paper which he had found tied to her coat.

◆

After a successful journey, Florizel, Perdita, Camillo and the old shepherd arrived safely at the court of Leontes. The king, who still felt deep grief for his dead wife and his lost child, received Camillo with great kindness, and gave a warm welcome to Prince Florizel. But it was Perdita, whom Florizel introduced as his princess, who seemed to attract all his attention. He saw that she looked like Hermione, and he said that his own daughter might have been such a lovely creature if he had not so cruelly destroyed her.

'And then, too,' he said to Florizel, 'I lost the society and friendship of your father, whom I now desire more than my life to see again.'

When the old shepherd heard how much notice the king had taken of Perdita, and how he had lost a daughter when she was only a baby, he began to compare the time when he had found the little Perdita, and the way in which she had been left to die. From all of this, the jewels and other signs of her high birth, he was forced to believe that Perdita was the king's lost daughter.

Florizel and Perdita, Camillo and the faithful Paulina were all present when the old shepherd told the king how he had found the child, and how he himself had seen Antigonus die.

He showed them the rich coat, in which Paulina remembered that Hermione had wrapped the child. He produced a jewel which Paulina remembered that Hermione had tied around the child's neck, and he gave up the paper on which Paulina recognized her husband's writing. It could not be doubted that Perdita was Leontes' own daughter.

Paulina was torn between sorrow for her husband's death and joy that the king's long-lost daughter had been found. When Leontes understood that Perdita was his daughter, his misery that Hermione was not alive to see her made him unable to say anything for a long time, except 'O your mother! Your mother!'

Paulina now told Leontes that she had had a statue made of Hermione which looked exactly like the queen. They all went with him to look at it. The king was anxious to see the statue of his Hermione, and Perdita was eager to see what her mother had looked like.

When Paulina pulled back the curtain which hid this statue, it looked so perfectly like Hermione that all the king's sorrow came back to him at the sight. For a long time he lost the power to speak or move.

'I like your silence, my lord,' said Paulina. 'It shows the strength of your feelings more than any words can. Is this statue not very like your queen?'

At last the king said, 'Oh, she stood like this when I first loved her. But, Paulina, Hermione was not as old as this statue looks.'

'Then the man who made the statue is a great artist,' Paulina replied, 'since he has made Hermione as she would have looked if she were living now. But let me pull the curtain, sir, in case soon you think it moves.'

The king then said, 'Do not pull the curtain. See, Camillo, do you not think it breathed? Her eye seems to have movement in it.'

'I must close the curtain, my lord,' Paulina said. 'You will persuade yourself the statue lives.'

'O, sweet Paulina,' said Leontes, 'I would like to believe that. But what instrument can cut breath from stone? Let no man laugh at me, for I am going to kiss her.'

'Stop, my lord!' said Paulina. 'The red on her lips is wet; you will mark your own with paint. Shall I close the curtain?'

'No, not for 20 years,' said Leontes.

All this time Perdita had been kneeling and looking, in silent admiration, at the statue of her mother. Now she said, 'And I could stay here for just as long, looking at my dear mother.'

'Either let me close the curtain,' said Paulina to Leontes, 'or prepare yourself for another surprise. I can make the statue move from where it stands and take you by the hand. But then you will think that I am helped by some evil powers, which I am not.'

'I am happy to watch what you can make her do,' said Leontes. 'It is as easy to make her speak as move.'

Paulina then ordered some slow music to be played, and to everyone's surprise, the statue came down and threw its arms around Leontes' neck. The statue then began to speak, praying for her husband, and her child, the newly found Perdita.

It was not surprising that the statue hung on Leontes's neck, and prayed for her husband and her child, because the statue was actually Hermione herself, the real and living queen.

Paulina had falsely reported to the king that Hermione was dead, thinking that it was the only way to save her life. Ever since then, Hermione had lived with the good Paulina. She had not wanted Leontes to know that she was alive until she heard that Perdita had been found; although she had forgiven the wrong that Leontes had done to her, she could not forgive his cruelty to his own baby daughter.

With his dead queen returned to life and his lost daughter found, Leontes could hardly bear the greatness of his own happiness.

Nothing but warm words and loving speeches were heard on all sides. The happy parents thanked Prince Florizel for loving their daughter when she had seemed to be of such low birth, and they thanked the good old shepherd for looking after their child. Camillo and Paulina were filled with joy because they had lived to see such a satisfactory end to all their faithful services.

And to complete this strange and unexpected joy, King Polixenes himself now entered the palace.

When Polixenes had first missed his son and Camillo, he had guessed that Camillo might have returned to Sicily. Following as quickly as he could, he arrived by chance at this, the happiest moment of Leontes' life.

Polixenes joined in the general joy. He forgave his friend Leontes for his unfair jealousy and they loved each other again with all the warmth of their early friendship. And now, of course, he was quite ready to agree to his son's marriage to Perdita, the future queen of Sicily.

So Hermione was rewarded for her long period of suffering. That excellent lady lived for many years with her Leontes and her Perdita, the happiest of mothers and of queens.

King Lear

Lear, King of Britain
King of France
Duke of Burgundy
Duke of Cornwall
Duke of Albany
Earl of Kent
Edgar, lawful son of the Earl of Gloucester
Edmund, natural son of the Earl of Gloucester
A Fool
Goneril ⎫
Regan   ⎬ daughters of King Lear
Cordelia ⎭

Lear, King of Britain, had three daughters – Goneril, wife of the Duke of Albany, Regan, wife of the Duke of Cornwall, and Cordelia, the youngest. The King of France and the Duke of Burgundy each wanted Cordelia for his wife, and at the time of this story they were staying at Lear's court.

The old king was over eighty years old and tired of government. He had decided to take no further part in state affairs, but to leave younger people to manage it. He called his three daughters to him to find out from their own lips which of them loved him best, so that he could divide his lands and money among them according to their love for him.

Goneril, the oldest, declared that she loved her father more than words could tell; that he was dearer to her than the light of her own eyes, dearer than life itself. Such talk is easy to pretend where there is no real love, but the king was very pleased to hear it. Thinking that her heart went with her words, he gave her and her husband one-third of his large kingdom.

Regan, his second daughter, who was as worthless as her sister, declared that the love which she felt for her father was much greater than her sister's. She found all other joys dead compared with the pleasure which she took in the love of her dear king and father.

Lear felt so happy to have what he thought were such loving children that he gave Regan and her husband another third of his kingdom, equal in size to the share which he had already given to Goneril.

Then turning to his youngest daughter, Cordelia, whom he called his joy, he asked what she had to say. He thought no doubt that she would please his ears with the same loving speeches as her sisters, or even that hers would be stronger than theirs, as she had always been his favourite. But Cordelia was upset by the claims made by her sisters, which she knew were only intended to persuade the king to give them part of his country. So she only answered that she loved her father according to her duty, neither more nor less.

The king was shocked at these words from his favourite child, and asked her to consider her words carefully and to improve her speech so that it did not spoil her fortunes.

Cordelia then told the king that she loved, obeyed and honoured him because he was her father and he had brought her up and loved her. But she could not make such grand speeches as her sisters had done or promise to love nothing else in the world. Why did her sisters have husbands if (as they said) they had no love for anything except their father? If she ever married, she was sure that her husband would want at least half of her love, half of her care and duty.

Cordelia really loved her father almost as much as her sisters pretended to do. At any other time, she would have told him so in stronger and more loving words. But when she saw how her sisters' deceitful words had won such rich prizes, she thought the best thing she could do was to love and be silent. This showed that she loved him, but not for what she could obtain, and her words, simple as they were, had much more truth and sincerity in them than those of her sisters.

Old age had made Lear so unwise that he could not tell truth from untruth, nor a brightly painted speech from words that came from the heart. He was so angry at Cordelia's plainness of speech, which he called pride, that he shared the third part of his kingdom equally between Cordelia's two sisters and their husbands, the Dukes of Albany and Cornwall. He now called them to him, and, in the presence of all his court, he gave them his kingdom to share, together with all the powers of government. He kept only the title of king for himself, and it was agreed that he, and a hundred soldiers to serve him, should live month by month in each of his daughters' palaces in turn.

Such an unbelievably foolish division of his country, made more in anger than by reason, filled all his nobles with shock and sorrow. But none of them had the courage to act except the Earl of Kent. He was beginning to speak for Cordelia when the angry Lear commanded him to stop or he would have him put to death. To this the good Kent paid no attention. He had always been faithful to Lear, whom he had honoured as a king, loved as a father and followed as a master. He had been ready to give his life in war against the king's enemies or when the king's safety was in danger. Now that Lear was his own greatest enemy, this faithful servant argued with him for Lear's own good.

He begged the king to follow his advice, as he had so often done in the past, and to undo what he had so unwisely done. Kent said that he would die rather than let Lear believe that his youngest daughter loved him less than her sisters did. As for Lear's threats, they could not frighten a man whose life was already at the king's service. That should not prevent him from speaking the truth.

The honest words of this good Earl of Kent only made the king more angry. Like a madman who kills his own doctor, he ordered this true servant to leave the country, and gave him only five days to prepare to do so. If, on the sixth day, he was found within the borders of Britain, he would be put to death.

So Kent said goodbye to the king, but before he went he called on the gods to protect Cordelia. He only hoped that her sisters' fine speeches would be followed by acts of love; and then he left, as he said, to carry his old life to a new country.

The King of France and the Duke of Burgundy were now called in to hear what Lear had decided about his youngest daughter, and to see whether they still wanted to marry Cordelia, now that she had nothing but herself to bring them. The Duke of Burgundy refused to have her as his wife under such conditions, but the King of France understood why she had lost her father's love. He took her by the hand and said that her goodness was worth more than a kingdom. He told her to say goodbye to her sisters and to her father, even though he had been unkind to her, and said that she should go with him and be his queen and rule over a fairer kingdom than her sisters.

Then, with tears in her eyes, Cordelia said goodbye to her sisters and begged them to love their father well. They told her that they knew their duty, and advised her to try to make her husband happy, for he had taken her almost as a beggar. And so Cordelia left, with a heavy heart, because she knew the deceit of her sisters and she wished that her father could be in better hands than theirs.

◆

As soon as Cordelia had gone, her sisters began to show their true characters. Even before the end of the first month, which Lear spent with his oldest daughter Goneril, the old king began to find out the difference between promises and actions. Once she had got from her father all that he had to give, the ungrateful woman now began to dislike the few small signs that showed he was still king. She could not bear to see him and his hundred soldiers. Every time she met her father, she was angry with him. When the old man wanted to speak to her, she pretended to be sick, so she did not have to see him. It was plain that she thought his old age a useless continuation of his life, and his soldiers an unnecessary cost. She stopped showing any respect to the king and, following her example and even her orders, her servants also began to ignore him; they refused to obey his orders or pretended not to hear him.

Lear could not help noticing this change in his daughter's behaviour, but he shut his eyes to it for as long as he could, just as most people do not wish to believe the unpleasant effects of their own mistakes.

All this time, the good Earl of Kent had chosen to stay in Britain as long as there was a chance of being useful to his master, although he knew that if he was discovered he would be put to death. Dressed as a servant, he offered his services to the king. The latter did not recognize him as Kent in his new dress, but was pleased with his direct speech and honesty; and so an agreement was made, and Lear took his favourite adviser back into his service under the name of Caius.

Caius quickly found a way to show his loyalty to his royal master. That same day one of Goneril's servants was disrespectful to Lear and spoke rudely to him, as no doubt he was secretly encouraged to do by Goneril herself. Caius quickly knocked him down, and Lear was grateful for his support.

Caius was not the only friend Lear had. It was the custom of kings at that time to keep a fool to make them laugh after finishing more serious business. The poor fool who had once lived in Lear's palace stayed with him after he had given away his kingdom, and often made him happy, although the man often laughed at Lear for his foolishness in giving away everything to his daughters.

Goneril now plainly told the king that he could not continue to stay in her palace if he still wished to keep his hundred soldiers. She said that such a number was both expensive and useless, and only filled her court with noise and feasting. She asked him to reduce the number and to keep only the old men, men like himself and suitable for his age.

At first Lear could not believe his eyes or ears. He could not believe that his own daughter would speak to him so unkindly.

But when she repeated her demand, the old man became angry and said she was lying. It is true that she was; the hundred soldiers were all men of polite behaviour and excellent manners who were not in the habit of making a noise.

Lear decided to go to his other daughter, Regan, taking his hundred soldiers with him, and he ordered his horses to be prepared. He spoke of Goneril's ungratefulness and prayed that she might never have a child, or, if she did, that it might live to show her the disrespect that she had shown to him. Then she would know that a thankless child is worse than the bite of a snake. The Duke of Albany began to make excuses for any share which Lear might think he had in the unkindness, but Lear refused to listen to him. He set out with his followers for Regan's house. He thought to himself how small Cordelia's fault (if it was a fault) now seemed, compared with her sister's, and he cried. Then he was ashamed that such a creature as Goneril had enough power over him to make him cry like this.

Regan and her husband were living in great style at their palace. Lear sent his servant Caius with letters to his daughter to prepare her for his arrival, while he and his soldiers followed. But Goneril too sent letters to her sister, saying that her father would do nothing he was asked and was bad-tempered, and advising Regan not to receive him with such a large number of followers.

This messenger arrived at the same time as Caius, and it was the servant whom Caius had formerly knocked down for his rude behaviour to Lear. Caius suspected what he had come for, and spoke angrily to him. He asked him to fight, but the servant refused. Caius then gave him a good beating, but when Regan and her husband heard of this, they ordered Caius to be publicly beaten and tied up in the square for everyone to see, even though he was a messenger from the king and should have been treated with respect. So the first thing the king saw when he entered the castle was his servant sitting in that shameful situation.

This was a bad sign of how he might expect to be received, but a worse one followed. When he asked for his daughter and her husband, he was told that they were very tired after travelling all night, and could not see him. He was angry and demanded to see them, but when at last they came to greet him, the hated Goneril was with them. She had come to tell her own story and set her sister against the king, her father.

The old man was very upset by this sight, and even more so when he saw Regan take Goneril by the hand. He asked Goneril if she was not ashamed to look at his white beard. Regan advised him to go home again with Goneril and live with her peacefully, sending away half his soldiers and asking her forgiveness. She said that he was old and lacking in good sense, and must be ruled by persons who had more wisdom than himself.

Lear asked if he should go down on his knees and beg for food and clothes from his own daughter. He said that he would never return with her but would stay with Regan, he and his hundred soldiers, for she had not forgotten the half of the kingdom which he had given her, and her eyes were not cold like Goneril's, but gentle and kind. He also said that rather than return to Goneril with only half his soldiers, he would go to France and beg help from the king who had married his youngest daughter when she had nothing.

But he was mistaken in thinking that he would receive kinder treatment from Regan than he had done from her sister Goneril. She now declared that she thought 50 soldiers were too many to wait on him, and that 25 were enough. Then Lear, nearly heartbroken, turned to Goneril and said that he would go back with her, for her 50 was double 25, and so her love was twice as much as Regan's. But Goneril excused herself and asked why he needed so many as twenty-five, or even ten, or even five, when her own servants or her sister's could look after him.

So these two ungrateful daughters each tried to be more cruel than the other to their old father, who had been so good to them. Their aim was gradually to rob him of all his soldiers and of all the respect that was left to show that he had once been a king. It was hard to change from a king to a beggar, and it was his daughters' ungratefulness which hurt this poor king so much. His mind began to become unbalanced and, though he did not know what he was saying, he promised that these unnatural creatures should be punished.

While he was threatening what his weak arm could never perform, night fell, and a fearful storm of thunder, lightning and rain began. His daughters still refused to let his followers enter, and Lear called for his horses, saying that he would rather face the greatest anger of the storm outside than stay under the same roof as these ungrateful daughters. Reminding him that the actions of foolish men bring their own just punishment, they let him go and shut their doors on him.

The wind was high, and the rain and the storm increased when the old man went out to struggle against them. For many miles there was hardly a bush for shelter. On a stretch of wasteland, King Lear wandered about, shouting in anger against the wind and the thunder. He commanded the wind to blow the earth into the sea, or to make the waves so big that they drowned the earth, so that no sign remained of such an ungrateful animal as man. The king was now left with no other companion than the fool, who still stayed with him. He tried to cheer the king up with his amusing words: he said it was a bad night for swimming, and that the king had better go and ask for his daughters' help.

This once great king was found in this condition by his ever-faithful servant the good Earl of Kent, now known as Caius. He said, 'O good sir, are you here? Creatures that love the night do not love such nights as these. This terrible storm has driven the animals to their hiding places. Man's nature cannot bear it.' But Lear reminded him that one does not feel smaller evils when there is a greater illness. When the mind is balanced, the body has time to feel ill, but the storm in his mind took away all other feeling from him. He spoke again of his daughters' disloyalty, and said it was as if the mouth tore the hand for lifting food to it; for parents were hands and food and everything to children.

Caius still continued to beg the king not to stay out in the open air, and at last persuaded him to enter a miserable little hut that they came to. The fool entered first but ran out in terror saying that he had seen a spirit. The spirit proved to be nothing but a poor beggar, who had gone into this hut for shelter and who had frightened the fool by talking about devils. When the king saw him, with only a cloth around his waist, he was sure that he was a man who had given away everything to his daughters. He believed that nothing could bring a man to such misery except unkind children.

From this, and from many wild speeches which he made, the good Caius saw clearly that Lear was not in his right mind, but that the cruel treatment he had suffered from his daughters had really made him mad.

The Earl of Kent's faithfulness now showed itself more clearly than it had ever done before. With the help of some of the king's soldiers, he had the king taken to the castle at Dover, where most of his own friends were. Kent himself set sail for France, where he hurried to Cordelia. He told her of her father's pitiful condition and how it had been caused by the cruelty of her sisters. This loving child begged her husband to let her go to England with an army big enough to defeat these cruel daughters and their husbands. The king agreed to this, so she set out with a royal army and landed at Dover.

Lear had escaped from the care of the soldiers in whose charge Kent had left him, and he was found by some of Cordelia's soldiers, wandering about the fields near Dover in a sad condition. He was quite mad, and singing aloud to himself, with a crown on his head which he had made of grass and other wild plants that he had picked up in the corn fields. Cordelia greatly desired to see her father, but the doctors persuaded her to delay the meeting until sleep and medicine had made him better. With the help of these skilful men, to whom Cordelia promised all her gold and jewels if they helped her father back to good health, Lear was soon in a condition to see his daughter.

It was a moving sight to see the meeting between the father and daughter. Lear was torn between his joy at seeing his child again and his shame at receiving such kindness from the daughter he had sent away in his foolish pride and anger. His half-mad brain sometimes made him unable to remember where he was, or who it was that kissed him so kindly. Then he would beg those who were with him not to laugh at him if he were mistaken in thinking this lady to be his daughter Cordelia. He fell on his knees to ask his daughter's forgiveness, but she, good lady, told him it was not a suitable thing for him to do. She was only doing her duty as she was his child. She kissed him (as she said) to kiss away all her sisters' unkindness, and said that they ought to be ashamed of themselves for turning their kind old father with his white beard out into the cold air. She would not have turned away her enemy's dog on a night like that, even if it had bitten her; it could have stayed by her fire and warmed itself.

Cordelia told her father that she had come from France to help him. He asked her to forgive and forget, since he was an old man and a foolish one and he did not know what he was doing. She certainly had good reason not to love him, but her sisters had no excuse. To this, Cordelia replied that she had no cause, and neither had they.

◆

We can leave this old king in the care of his loving child. With the help of sleep and medicine, she and her doctors at last succeeded in bringing some peace to that troubled mind, which was so upset by the cruelty of his other daughters. Let us now go back to say a word or two about them.

These ungrateful creatures, who had been so false to their own father, could not be expected to be more faithful to their husbands. They soon grew tired of showing even the appearance of love and duty, and made it clear that they had given their love to another man. And each of them fell in love with the same man. It was Edmund, a natural son of the dead Earl of Gloucester. By his evil actions, he had removed his brother Edgar, the lawful heir, from his possessions, and was now earl himself.

At about this time the Duke of Cornwall, Regan's husband, died. Regan at once declared her intention of marrying this Earl of Gloucester. This excited the jealousy of her sister, to whom the evil earl had spoken of his love, and Goneril killed Regan by giving her poison. But Goneril's husband discovered what she had done and put her in prison, where she soon put an end to her own life. In this way the justice of heaven at last claimed these ungrateful daughters.

But a sad end was waiting for Cordelia, whose kindness seemed to deserve better fortune. The armies which Goneril and Regan had sent out under the command of Edmund, the bad Earl of Gloucester, were successful. They caught Cordelia and she was taken to prison and killed there. Lear did not live long after his sweet child's death.

Before the king died, the good Earl of Kent tried to tell him that it was he who had followed him under the name of Caius. Lear's troubled brain could not understand how that could be, or how Kent and Caius could be the same person, so Kent thought it unnecessary to try to explain. This faithful servant to the king died of grief soon after his master.

There is no need here to tell how the bad Earl of Gloucester was killed in a fight with his brother, or how Goneril's husband, the Duke of Albany, who had never encouraged his lady in her bad ways, became the King of England. Lear and his three daughters are dead, and our story ends with them.

The Taming of the Shrew

Katharine was the oldest daughter of Baptista, a rich gentleman of Padua. She was a lady with such an ungovernable temper and such a loud and angry tongue that she was known in Padua by no other name than Katharine the Shrew. It seemed unlikely, even impossible, that any gentleman would ever be found who would dare to marry this lady. So Baptista was much criticized because he refused to give his agreement to many excellent offers that were made to her gentle sister, Bianca, saying that until the oldest sister was married, young Bianca would not be free to take a husband.

But it happened that a gentleman named Petruchio came to Padua with the aim of looking for a wife. Not being discouraged by these accounts of Katharine's temper, and hearing that she was rich and beautiful, he was determined to marry this famous shrew and to tame her into a gentle wife who would obey him.

No one was so suitable to attempt this as Petruchio. He was as spirited as Katharine and he was an amusing and good-natured person. He was also clever and wise enough to know how to pretend to be angry and cold when he was in fact so calm that he could have laughed happily at his own ability to pretend. So Petruchio went to make love to Katharine the Shrew. First of all he begged Baptista's permission to try to win his *gentle* daughter Katharine, as Petruchio called her, as his wife. He said that, having heard of her gentle behaviour, he had come from Verona to ask for her love. Though her father wished her to be married, he was forced to admit that Katharine's character was quite different from this. What gentleness she had soon became very clear, when her music teacher rushed into the room to complain that his pupil had hit him over the head with her instrument because he had dared to find fault with her performance.

When Petruchio heard this, he said, 'What an excellent lady! I love her more than ever, and only want to talk to her.' Begging her father to agree to this, he said, 'I am in a hurry, sir; I cannot come every day to try to win her. You knew my father: he is dead, and has left me heir to all his lands and goods. Tell me, if I win your daughter's love, what money you will give with her.'

Baptista thought his manner was rather rough for a lover, but because he would be glad to get Katharine married, he answered that he would give her twenty thousand crowns and half his possessions on his death. So this strange marriage was quickly agreed to, and Baptista went to tell his shrewish daughter that she had a lover, and sent her in to Petruchio to listen to his lovemaking.

While this was happening, Petruchio was deciding on the way in which he would tell her of his love. He said, 'If she is angry with me, I will tell her that she sings as sweetly as a bird; and if she looks cross, I will say she looks as clear as roses newly washed with rain. If she will not speak a word, I will praise the beauty of her language; and if she tells me to leave her, I will thank her as if she had asked me to stay with her for a week.'

Katharine now entered, and Petruchio spoke to her.

'Good morning, Kate, for that is your name, I hear.'

Katharine, not liking this greeting, said proudly, 'Those who speak to me call me Katharine.'

'You lie,' replied the lover, 'for you are called plain Kate, and pretty Kate, and sometimes Kate the Shrew, but, Kate, you are the prettiest Kate in all the world, and so, Kate, hearing your gentleness praised in every town, I have come to win you for my wife.'

In loud and angry words, she showed him how she had gained the name of Shrew, while he still continued to praise her sweet language. At last, hearing her father coming and intending to be as quick as possible, he said, 'Sweet Katharine, let us stop; your father has agreed that you shall be my wife, and whether you wish it or not, I will marry you.'

Now Baptista entered and Petruchio told him that his daughter had received him kindly, and that she had promised to marry him the following Sunday. Katharine said that this was untrue; she would rather see him hanged on Sunday, she said, and she blamed her father for wishing to marry her to a madman like Petruchio. Petruchio asked her father not to pay attention to her angry words, since they had agreed that she would seem against the marriage in his presence, but when they were alone he had found her very loving.

He said to her, 'Give me your hand, Kate; I will go to Venice to buy you fine clothes for our marriage. Provide the feast, Father, and invite the guests. I will be sure to bring rings and expensive dresses so that my Kate may be beautiful. And kiss me, Kate, because we will be married on Sunday.'

◆

On the Sunday all the wedding guests were together, but they had to wait a long time before Petruchio came. As they waited, Katharine cried, annoyed to think that Petruchio had only been making fun of her. At last he appeared, but he brought none of the fine clothes which he had promised Katharine. Nor was he himself dressed like a man about to be married, but in a strange, untidy way, as if he intended to make fun of the serious business he came to do. Even his servant and the horses they rode were clothed in the same poor and strange manner.

Petruchio could not be persuaded to change his dress. He said that Katharine was to be married to him, and not to his clothes. Finding it useless to argue with him, she went with him to church. Here, he still behaved in the same mad way. When the priest asked Petruchio if he wanted Katharine to be his wife, he said so loudly that he did that the shocked priest dropped his book; as he bent down to pick it up, this crazy man gave him such a blow that both the priest and his book fell down again. And all the time they were being married, he stamped his feet and shouted, so that the high-spirited Katharine trembled and shook with fear.

After the ceremony was over, while they were still in the church, Petruchio called for wine and loudly drank the company's health. Then he threw the rest of his drink into the face of one of the men there, giving no other reason for this strange act except that the man's beard looked thin and hungry and seemed to need the wine to make it grow. There had never been a madder wedding; but Petruchio was only pretending to be mad so that he would be more successful in the plan he had formed to tame his shrewish wife.

Baptista had provided an expensive wedding feast, but when they returned from church, Petruchio said that it was his intention to take his wife home immediately. Neither the arguments of his wife's father nor Katharine's angry words could make him change his mind. He claimed a husband's right to do what he pleased with his wife, and hurried Katharine away, seeming so determined that no one dared attempt to stop him.

Petruchio put his wife on a thin and hungry-looking horse, which he had specially chosen for her, and he and his servant had no better ones. They travelled along rough and muddy paths, and whenever Katharine's horse seemed about to fall, he would shout at the poor tired horse, which could hardly move under its load.

At last, after a tiring journey, during which Katharine had heard nothing but Petruchio's shouting at the servant and the horses, they arrived at his house. Petruchio welcomed her kindly to her home, but he had made up his mind that she should have neither food nor rest that night. The tables were spread and supper soon served, but Petruchio pretended to find fault with every dish. He threw the meat on the floor, and ordered the servants to take it away. All this he did, as he said, in love for his Katharine, so that she did not have to eat meat that was not well cooked. And when Katharine went to rest, tired and supperless, he found the same fault with the bed; he threw the bedclothes around the room so that she was forced to sit down in a chair. If she fell asleep, she was quickly awoken by her husband's loud voice, as he shouted at the servants for making his wife's marriage bed so badly.

The next day Petruchio continued to act in the same way. He still spoke kind words to Katharine, but when she attempted to eat, he found fault with everything that was put in front of her and threw the breakfast on the floor as he had done the supper. Katharine, proud Katharine, was forced to beg the servants to bring her food secretly, but they had already been given their orders by Petruchio and replied that they dared not give her anything without their master's knowledge.

'Oh!' Katharine said to herself. 'Did he marry me to keep me hungry? Beggars that come to my father's door are given

29

food. But I, who never knew what it was to beg for anything, am kept without food and without sleep. He keeps me awake and feeds me with his shouting. And, which makes me more angry, he does it all in the name of perfect love.'

Her thoughts were interrupted by the entrance of Petruchio. He had brought her a small piece of meat, and he said to her, 'How is my sweet Kate? See, love, how much I think of you. I have cooked your meat myself. I am sure this kindness deserves thanks. What, not a word? Then you do not love the meat, and all the trouble I have taken is for nothing.' He then ordered the servant to take the dish away.

Her great hunger had lessened Katharine's pride and, though she was still very angry, she said, 'I beg you, leave it here.'

But Petruchio intended to make her obey him more readily than this, and he replied, 'The poorest service is repaid with thanks, and so shall mine be before you touch the meat.'

So Katharine said with difficulty, 'I thank you, sir.'

Now he let her have a very small meal, saying, 'May it do your gentle heart much good, Kate; eat it all quickly. And now, my love, we will return to your father's house, and show ourselves as finely dressed as the best, with silk coats and caps and golden rings.'

To make her believe that he really intended to give her these beautiful things, he called in a dressmaker and a hat-maker, who brought some new clothes he had ordered for her. Then he gave her plate to the servant to take away before she had half satisfied her hunger.

The hat-maker showed a cap, saying, 'Here is the cap you ordered.' At this, Petruchio began to shout again, saying that the cap was no bigger than a nutshell and telling the hat-maker to take it away and make it bigger.

Katharine said, 'I will have this; all gentlewomen wear caps like these.'

'When you are gentle,' replied Petruchio, 'you shall have one too, and not until then.'

The food Katharine had eaten had made her a little stronger, and she said, 'Well, sir, I hope I may be allowed to speak, and I *will* speak. I am not a child; better people than you have heard me say what I think, and if you cannot, you had better close your ears.'

Petruchio refused to listen to these angry words, since he had happily discovered a better way of managing his wife than having an argument with her. So his answer was: 'Ah, you speak the truth. It is a poor and worthless cap, and I love you because you do not like it.'

'Love me, or love me not,' said Katharine, 'I like the cap, and I will have this cap or none at all.'

'You say you wish to see the dress,' said Petruchio, still pretending to misunderstand her.

The dressmaker then came forward and showed her a fine dress which she had made for her. Petruchio, who intended that she should have neither cap nor dress, found as much fault with that, saying that the material was poor and that the dress was badly cut.

The dressmaker said, 'You told me to make it according to the fashion of the time.' And Katharine herself said that she had never seen a better-made dress.

This was enough for Petruchio. Having given private orders that these people should be paid for their goods, and that excuses should be made to them for the strange treatment he had given them, he ordered the dressmaker and the hat-maker out of the room. Then, turning to Katharine, he said, 'Well, come, my Kate, we will just go to your father's house in these poor clothes which we are wearing now.' Then he ordered his horses, saying that they would reach Baptista's home by dinnertime, as it was only seven o'clock.

Now it was not in fact early morning when he said this, but the middle of the day. So Katharine dared to say, though politely, since she was almost overcome by his forceful manner, 'But sir, I tell you it is two o'clock, and it will be suppertime before we get there.'

Petruchio intended that she should be so completely tamed, before he took her to see her father, that she would agree to everything he said. Therefore, as if he were lord even of the sun, and could command the hours, he said it would be whatever time he pleased before he started on the journey. 'Because,' he said, 'whatever I say or do, you are still going against it. I will not go today, and when I go, it will be the time I say it is.'

◆

Katharine was forced to practise obeying her husband for another day, since Petruchio would not let her go to her father's house until she had learned to obey him without question. Even while they were on their journey there, she was in danger of being turned back again, only because she suggested that it was the sun when he declared that the moon was shining brightly at midday.

'Now, by my mother's son,' he said, 'and that is myself, it will be the moon, or stars, or what I wish, before I travel to your father's house.'

He then acted as if he were going back again, but Katharine – no longer Katharine the Shrew, but the obedient wife – said, 'Let us go on, please, now that we have come so far. It can be the sun, or moon, or what you please, and if you want to call it something else, I promise you that is what it will be for me.'

Petruchio was determined to prove this, and so he said again, 'I say it is the moon.'

'I know it is the moon,' replied Katharine.

'You lie; it is the sun,' said Petruchio.

'Then it is the sun,' replied Katharine. 'But it is not the sun when you say it is not. Whatever you wish to call it, that is what it is, and what it always will be for Katharine.'

Now he allowed her to continue on her journey. But in order to see if this obedience would last, he spoke to an old gentleman they met on the road as if he were a young woman, saying to him, 'Good day, gentle lady.' He asked Katharine if she had ever seen a fairer woman, praising the red and white of the old man's cheeks, and comparing his eyes to two bright stars. He spoke to him again, saying, 'Fair, lovely lady, once more good day to you!' and said to his wife, 'Sweet Kate, take her in your arms. She is so beautiful.'

Katharine, by now completely tamed, quickly made her speech in the same manner to the old gentleman, saying to him, 'Young lady, you are fair, and fresh, and sweet. Where are you going, and where is your home? The parents of so fair a child must be very happy.'

'Why, Kate, what is this?' said Petruchio. 'I hope you are not mad. This is a man, old and lined, and not a young lady as you say he is.'

At this, Katharine said, 'Forgive me, old gentleman. The sun has blinded my eyes. Now I can see that you are truly a respected father. I hope you will forgive me for my sad mistake.'

'Do, good old man,' said Petruchio, 'and tell us which way you are travelling. We shall be glad to have your company if you are going our way.'

The old gentleman, much shocked at the manner in which these two had spoken to him, replied, 'My name is Vincentio, and I am going to visit a son of mine who lives in Padua.'

Then Petruchio knew that the old gentleman was the father of Lucentio, a young man who was going to be married to Baptista's younger daughter, Bianca. He made Vincentio very happy by telling him of the rich marriage his son was about to make, and they all travelled on pleasantly together until they came to Baptista's house. Here a large company was present for the marriage of Bianca and Lucentio, since Baptista had happily agreed to it after Katharine was married. When they entered, Baptista welcomed them to the celebrations.

There was also another newly married pair at the ceremony. Lucentio, Bianca's husband, and Hortensio, the other newly married man, could not stop themselves from making fun of Petruchio's shrewish wife. These men seemed very pleased with the gentle natures of the ladies they had chosen, and laughed at Petruchio for his less fortunate choice. Petruchio took little notice of their amusement until the ladies had left the room after dinner, and then he saw that Baptista himself had joined in the laughter against him. When Petruchio declared that his wife would prove more obedient than theirs, Katharine's father said, 'Now, in all sadness, son Petruchio, I fear you have got the worst shrew of all.'

'Well,' said Petruchio, 'I say I have not. So, to prove that I speak the truth, let us each one send for his wife, and he whose wife is most obedient and comes most quickly when she is sent for, shall win a bet which we will agree on.'

The other two husbands were quite ready to do this, for they were sure that their gentle wives would prove more obedient than the difficult Katharine. They suggested a bet of twenty crowns, but Petruchio said that he would bet as much as that on one of his dogs, and twenty times as much on his wife. Lucentio and Hortensio raised the bet to a hundred crowns, and Lucentio sent his servant to ask Bianca to come to him.

Soon the servant returned, and said, 'Sir, my lady sends you word that she is busy and cannot come.'

'What!' said Petruchio. 'Does she say that she is busy and cannot come? Is that an answer for a wife?'

Then they laughed at him and said he would be lucky if

Katharine did not send a worse answer.

Now it was Hortensio's turn to send for his wife, and he said to his servant, 'Go, and beg my wife to come to me.'

'Oh, *beg* her!' said Petruchio. 'Then she *must* come.'

'I am afraid, sir,' said Hortensio, 'your wife will not even come if you beg her to do so.'

But soon this loving husband looked a little unhappy, when the servant returned without his wife.

'Sir,' said the servant, 'my lady says that you are only having fun, and so she will not come. You can go to her instead.'

'Worse and worse!' said Petruchio. Then he sent his servant, saying, 'Go to my wife and tell her that I command her to come.'

The company had hardly had time to think that she would not obey this order, when Baptista said in surprise, 'By heavens, here comes Katharine!'

She entered, saying quietly to Petruchio, 'What is your wish, sir? Why have you sent for me?'

'Where are your sister and Hortensio's wife?' he asked.

'They are talking by the sitting-room fire,' Katharine replied.

'Go, bring them here!' said Petruchio.

Katharine went away without answering to perform her husband's command.

'This is a most surprising thing,' said Lucentio.

'And so it is,' said Hortensio, 'I cannot imagine what it means.'

'It means peace,' said Petruchio, 'and love, and a quiet life, and that I am the master. And, in short, everything that is sweet and happy.'

Katharine's father was filled with joy to see the change in his daughter, and said, 'Now, may fortune go with you, son Petruchio! You have won the bet, and I will add another twenty thousand crowns to what I gave her before, as if she were another daughter, because she is so changed that I hardly know her.'

'No,' said Petruchio, 'I will win the bet even more surely, and show more signs of her new goodness and obedience.'

Katharine now entered with the two ladies, and he continued, 'See how she brings the wives who disobey you as prisoners to her womanly persuasion. Katharine, that cap of yours does not suit you. Take it off, and throw it on the floor.'

Katharine immediately took off her cap and threw it down.

'Lord!' said Hortensio's wife. 'I hope I may never be made to do anything so silly.'

And Bianca said, 'What foolish duty do you call this?'

At this, Bianca's husband said to her, 'I wish your duty were as foolish too! The wisdom of your duty, fair Bianca, has cost me a hundred crowns since dinnertime.'

'Then you are foolish, too,' said Bianca, 'for betting on my duty.'

'Katharine,' said Petruchio, 'tell these women what duty they owe their lords and husbands.'

Then, to the surprise of all those present, Katharine spoke of the importance of obeying your husband. And Katharine once more became famous in Padua – not as before, as Katharine the Shrew, but as Katharine, the most obedient wife in Padua.

Romeo and Juliet

The two chief families in Verona were the rich Capulets and the Montagues. There had been an old quarrel between these families, and they were now such enemies that even their followers and servants could not meet without angry words which sometimes caused blood to flow. The noisy arguments that resulted from these accidental meetings often upset the peace of Verona's streets.

Old Lord Capulet gave a great supper, to which many fair ladies and noble lords were invited. All the beautiful women of Verona were present, and everyone else was made welcome if they were not of the house of Montague.

Rosaline, a lady loved by Romeo, who was the son of old Lord Montague, was present at this Capulet feast. Although it was dangerous for a Montague to be seen in this company, Benvolio, a friend of Romeo, persuaded the young lord to go with his face masked, a common fashion of the day at parties, so that he could see his Rosaline and compare her with some of the other lovely women of Verona, who (Benvolio said) would make her seem less beautiful.

Romeo did not much believe in Benvolio's words, but he was persuaded to go because of his love for Rosaline. Romeo was a faithful lover, who often could not sleep for thinking of Rosaline, and sometimes left the company of others just to be alone. But she showed little respect for him, and never returned his love, so Benvolio wished to cure his friend of this love by showing him a variety of other ladies.

So young Romeo went with Benvolio and their friend Mercutio to this party of the Capulets, with masks on their faces. They were welcomed by old Capulet himself, who told them that there were plenty of ladies for them to dance with. They began dancing, and Romeo was suddenly struck by the great beauty of a lady who danced there. She seemed to him to teach the lamps to burn more brightly; she was like a white bird among black ones (he said), in the way that her beauty and perfections shone above all other ladies.

While he was speaking these words of praise, Tybalt, a nephew of Lord Capulet, heard him by chance and knew by his voice that it was Romeo. Tybalt had a quick and angry temper, and could not bear that a Montague should come masked to make fun of them in their own home. He cried out in anger, and wanted to strike young Romeo dead. But his uncle, old Lord Capulet, would not let him harm Romeo at that time, both from respect for his guests and because Romeo had behaved like a gentleman. Tybalt, forced to be patient against his will, controlled himself, but declared that this evil Montague should pay at another time for his uninvited entrance.

When the dancing was finished, Romeo watched the place where the lady stood. The mask covering his face might seem to excuse a little the freedom with which he went up to her and, gently taking her by the hand, spoke to her in loving whispers while looking deep into her eyes. Though her replies were those of a lady, her heart was shaken and moved by the sight of this young man.

When the lady was called away to her mother, Romeo asked who her mother was. He then discovered that the lady whose perfect beauty had so greatly struck him was young Juliet, daughter and heir of the Lord Capulet, the great enemy of the Montagues – and to her, unknowingly, he had given his heart. This troubled him, but it could not prevent him from loving her. Juliet, too, had little rest when she found that the gentleman to whom she had been talking was Romeo and a Montague, since she had been struck with the same sudden and unthinking love for him as he had felt for her. It seemed to her a perfect birth of love, that she should love her enemy when, for family reasons alone, she ought to hate him.

◆

At midnight, Romeo left with his companions. But they soon missed him; he was unable to stay away from the house where he had left his heart, and he climbed over a wall into a garden which was at the back of Juliet's house. He had not been here long, thinking of his new love, when Juliet appeared above him at a window. Her great beauty seemed to break like the light of the sun in the east.

The moon, which shone in the garden with a faint light, appeared to Romeo to be sick and pale with grief at the greater brightness of this new sun. And when Juliet rested her face on her hand, he wished that he was a ring on that hand so that he could touch her. At the same time, thinking that she was alone, Juliet whispered, 'Ah me!'

Romeo answered softly, so that she could not hear, 'O speak again, bright angel, for that is how you appear, standing above me, like a messenger from heaven whom ordinary men step back to look at.'

She did not know that Romeo was there, but was full of the new love which that night had brought to her, and called on her lover by name, 'O Romeo, Romeo!' she said, 'Why are you called Romeo? Leave your father and refuse your name; or, if you will not, be my love, and I will no longer be a Capulet.'

With this encouragement, Romeo was eager to speak, but he wanted to hear more. The lady continued her talk of love to herself (as she thought), still blaming Romeo for being Romeo and a Montague, and wishing that he had some other name, since he could then be hers.

At this, Romeo could no longer prevent himself from speaking. As if her words had been addressed to him in person, and not only in her imagination, he begged her to call him Love, or by any other name she liked – he would no longer be Romeo, if that name did not please her.

Juliet, frightened at hearing a man's voice in the garden, did not at first know who it was who had learned her secret under the cover of night and darkness. But when he spoke again, and although her ears had not yet heard a hundred words of his, she knew immediately that it was Romeo. She blamed him for the danger into which he had put himself by climbing the garden wall; if any of her family found him there, they would kill him, because he was a Montague.

'Oh,' said Romeo, 'there is more danger in your eye than in 20 of their swords. If you look with kindness on me, lady, I am safe from my enemies. It would be better if my life were ended by their hate than that I should live longer without your love.'

'How did you come into this place,' said Juliet, 'and who guided you?'

'Love guided me,' answered Romeo.

Juliet's face became red when she remembered how she had made known her love for Romeo, without meaning to do so. She would have taken back her words, but that was impossible. She would have followed custom and kept her lover at a distance, as wise ladies do, so that their lovers may not think that they have been won too easily. But in her case, it was useless to pretend. Romeo had heard an admission of her love from her own tongue, when she did not know that he was near her. So, with perfect honesty, she told him that what he had heard before was true. Calling him by the name of "fair Montague" (since love can sweeten a sour name), she begged him not to think that she treated love lightly. Her behaviour might not seem wise, but it was more honest than the behaviour of women whose wisdom and shyness were only a clever pretence.

Romeo was beginning to call the heavens to be his witness that he could never think so dishonourably about such an honoured lady, when she stopped him, begging him not to speak such words. Although she found great happiness in him, she said that their promises that night were unwise and too sudden. When he demanded that they should exchange more serious promises of love, she said that she had given him hers before he asked for it. But she would take back again what she had given, so that she could have the pleasure of giving it again, because her kindness was as endless as the sea, and her love as deep.

Juliet was called away from this loving meeting by her nurse, who thought it was time for her to be in bed. But she quickly returned and said that if his love was really honourable and he wished to marry her, she would send a messenger to him the next day to fix a time for their marriage. Then she would lay all her fortunes at his feet, and follow him as her lord through the world.

While they were arranging this, she was called for again and again by her nurse, and went in and returned, and went and returned again. She seemed as jealous of Romeo going from her as he seemed unable to part from his Juliet; for the sweetest music to lovers is the sound of each other's tongue at night. But at last they parted, hoping for sweet sleep and rest.

◆

The day was now breaking. Romeo, whose mind was too full of thoughts of his love to let him sleep, went to find Friar Lawrence instead of going home. The good friar was already saying his morning prayers, and when he saw Romeo out so early and guessed that he had not been to bed all night, he thought – wrongly – that his love for Rosaline had kept him awake. But when Romeo told him of his new love for Juliet, and asked the friar's help to marry them that day, the man lifted up his hands and eyes in shock at the sudden change in Romeo. He had known all about Romeo's love for Rosaline, and his many complaints of her coldness to him; now the friar said that young men's love appeared not to lie in their hearts, but in their eyes.

Romeo replied that he had often blamed himself for thinking so much about Rosaline when she could not love him in return, but that Juliet both loved and was loved by him. The good friar thought that a marriage between young Juliet and Romeo might happily put an end to the long quarrel between the Capulets and the Montagues. Therefore, as he was a friend of both the families, and also as he greatly liked young Romeo, the old man agreed to perform the ceremony.

So when Juliet's messenger arrived, according to her promise, Romeo sent back a message with him, telling her to come quickly to Friar Lawrence's room. The good friar prayed that the heavens would smile on that act, and that the union of this young Montague and young Capulet would end for ever the old quarrel between their families.

When the ceremony was over, Juliet hurried home. There she waited impatiently for the coming of night, when Romeo had promised to come and meet her in the garden, where they had met the night before. The time seemed to pass as slowly to her as it does the night before a great celebration to an impatient child who has new clothes which it may not wear until the morning.

◆

That same morning, Romeo's friends Benvolio and Mercutio were walking through the streets of Verona, when they met a number of the Capulets, with Tybalt among them. This was the same Tybalt who had wanted to fight with Romeo at old Lord Capulet's supper. Seeing Mercutio, he criticized him for being a friend of Romeo, a Montague. Mercutio, who had as much anger and youthful blood in him as Tybalt, replied angrily to this. In spite of everything Benvolio could do to prevent it, a quarrel was beginning, but at that moment Romeo himself passed by. The angry Tybalt turned his attention from Mercutio to Romeo, and swore at him.

Romeo had no wish to quarrel with Tybalt, because he was a relation of Juliet and much loved by her. Besides, this young Montague had never completely entered into the family quarrel, since he was wise and gentle by nature. So he tried to make peace with Tybalt, whom he greeted by the name of "good Capulet", as if he, though a Montague, had some secret pleasure in speaking that name. But Tybalt, who hated all Montagues above everything, would not listen to him, and pulled out his sword.

Mercutio did not know of Romeo's secret reason for wanting peace with Tybalt, and thought his manner was a kind of dishonour. So with many disrespectful words, he forced Tybalt to fight him first. They fought until Mercutio was wounded and fell, while Romeo and Benvolio tried unsuccessfully to separate the fighters.

When Romeo realized that Mercutio was dead, he lost his temper and called Tybalt by the same insulting names that Tybalt had given him. They fought until Tybalt was killed by Romeo.

The news of this quarrel quickly spread and brought a crowd of people to the place, among whom were the old Lords Capulet and Montague with their wives. Soon afterwards, the Prince of Verona himself arrived. He was a relation of Mercutio, whom Tybalt had killed, and, as the peace of his government had often been upset by these quarrels, he came determined to punish severely those who had done wrong.

Benvolio, who had seen the fight, was ordered by the prince to tell him how it had begun. He did so, keeping as near to the truth as he could without doing harm to Romeo, and trying to excuse the part which his friends had played in it.

Lady Capulet, whose grief for the loss of Tybalt made her want nothing except revenge, begged the prince to see that justice was done to his murderer, and to pay no attention to Benvolio; since Benvolio was Romeo's friend and a Montague, naturally he spoke for him. In this way she argued against the man who, unknown to her, was now Juliet's husband.

On the other side was Lady Montague, begging for her child's life. She said, with some justice, that Romeo had done nothing for which he ought to be punished when he took the life of Tybalt who had himself first killed Mercutio.

Moved by the arguments of these women, the prince gave his judgement after a careful examination of the facts, and Romeo was ordered to leave Verona.

This was sad news for young Juliet, who had been a wife for only a few hours, and now, by this order, seemed to be separated from her husband for ever! When the news reached her, she was at first very angry with Romeo, who had killed her dear cousin. But in the end love won over hate, and the tears of grief that she cried because Romeo had killed her cousin turned to tears of joy because her husband, whom Tybalt had wanted to kill, was still alive. Then came fresh tears of grief when she remembered that Romeo had been sent away from her. That punishment was more terrible to bear than the death of many Tybalts.

◆

After the fight, Romeo had taken shelter with Friar Lawrence. Here he was first told of the prince's judgement, which seemed much more terrible than death. It seemed to him that there was no world outside Verona's walls, no life out of the sight of Juliet. Heaven was there where Juliet lived, and everything else was pain or punishment or death. The good friar tried to comfort the young man in his grief, but Romeo would not listen to him. Like a madman, he tore his hair, and threw himself down on the ground – to check the measurements of his grave, so he said.

He was brought to his senses a little by a message from his dear lady, and then the friar began to blame him for the unmanly weakness which he had shown. Romeo had killed Tybalt, the friar said, but did he also want to kill himself and his dear lady, who lived only for him? The law had been kind to him, since, instead of death, it had only ordered him to be sent away. He had killed Tybalt, but Tybalt would have killed him; there was a sort of happiness in that. Juliet was alive and had become his wife, so he ought to be very happy. And the friar told him to take care – those who lost all hope died miserable.

When Romeo was calm again, the friar advised him to go that night and say goodbye secretly to Juliet. Then he should go straight to Mantua, where he should stay until the friar found a suitable time to make the news of his marriage public, which might be a joyful way of making the two families friends again. Then he was sure that the prince would forgive Romeo, and he would return with 20 times more happiness than the grief with which he went away.

Persuaded by the friar's wise advice, Romeo said goodbye to him to go and see his lady. He planned to stay with her that night, and to make his journey alone to Mantua the following day. The good friar promised to send him letters there from time to time, telling him how things were at home.

Romeo passed that night with his dear wife, gaining entrance to her room from the garden in which he had heard her words of love the night before. That had been a night of complete joy and pleasure, but the happiness of the lovers this night was saddened by the thought that they must soon part. The unwelcome daylight seemed to come too soon, and the morning birdsong seemed to them a most unpleasant sound.

Soon the light of day in the east showed too certainly that it was time for these lovers to part, and Romeo sadly said goodbye to his dear wife, promising to write to her from Mantua at every hour in the day. When he had climbed down from her window, as he stood below her on the ground, Juliet thought sadly that he seemed like someone lying dead at the bottom of a grave. Romeo felt much the same; but now he was forced to leave, since it was death for him to be found inside the walls of Verona after the day had begun.

◆

This was only the beginning of the miserable story of this pair of unfortunate lovers. Romeo had not been gone for many days before Lord Capulet planned a marriage for Juliet. The man he had chosen for her, never thinking that she was married already, was Paris, a brave, young and noble gentleman, who would have been a very suitable husband for young Juliet if she had never seen Romeo.

Juliet was in a state of frightened confusion at her father's plans. At first she said that she was too young to marry; then, that the recent death of Tybalt had left her spirits too weak to be happy for a husband, and that it would not be right for the Capulets to have a marriage celebration when Tybalt had only just been buried. She gave every reason she could think of against the marriage, except the true one – that she was married already.

But old Lord Capulet would not listen to her excuses, and sharply ordered her to get ready; he had decided that by the next Thursday she should be married to Paris. Having found her a husband who was rich, young and noble enough for the proudest lady in Verona, he could not bear that her grief, as he thought it, should put difficulties in the way of her own good fortune.

Juliet now went to the old friar to beg him to help her out of the terrible position in which she found herself. He asked her if she was brave enough to carry out a dangerous plan, to which she replied that she would go into the grave alive rather than marry Paris while her own dear husband was living. Then the friar told her to go home and appear happy, and say that she was prepared to marry Paris as her father wished. On the next night, which was the night before the marriage, she must drink some medicine, which he then gave her. The effect of this would be that for 42 hours after drinking it she would appear cold and lifeless. When her future husband came to collect her in the morning, he would think that she was dead. Then she would be carried to the family grave to be buried. The friar said that if she could forget her womanly fears and agree to do this, she would be sure to be awake, as if from a dream, in 42 hours after swallowing the liquid. Before she woke, he would let her husband know what they had done, and Romeo would come in the night and take her away to Mantua. Love, and the fear of marrying Paris, gave young Juliet the strength to promise to do this terrible thing, and she left the friar, taking his medicine with her.

On her way back, she met young Paris, and, quietly pretending, promised to become his wife. This was joyful news to the Capulets. It seemed to make the old man young again, and Juliet, who had greatly displeased him by her refusal of Paris, became his dearest child again now that she promised to be obedient. Everybody in the house began to prepare for the coming marriage. A large amount of money was spent to provide for such a celebration as Verona had never seen before.

On the Wednesday night, Juliet drank the liquid. She had many doubts before she did so. She thought that the friar might have given her poison to avoid being blamed for marrying her to Romeo; then she remembered that he had always been known as a good, religious man. She feared that she might wake before the time that Romeo could come for her, and that in that terrible grave she might be driven mad. She thought of all the stories she had heard of spirits coming back to visit the places where their bodies were buried. But then her love for Romeo and her refusal to marry Paris returned; she swallowed the medicine and became unconscious.

When young Paris came early in the morning, he found a lifeless body instead of a living Juliet. What death to his hopes! What confusion there was then through the whole house! Poor Paris was full of grief for the woman whom death had robbed him of even before they had become man and wife. But it was still more pitiful to see the sadness of old Lord and Lady Capulet. They had only this one child to love and find comfort in, but cruel death had taken her from their sight just as she was about to make a good marriage. Now all the things that were ready for the celebration would have to serve for a funeral. Now, instead of a priest to marry her, a priest was needed to bury her. She was carried to church, not to increase the cheerful hopes of the living, but to swell the cheerless numbers of the dead.

◆

Bad news always travels faster than good. Romeo, in Mantua, heard the sad story of his Juliet's death before Friar Lawrence's messenger could arrive to tell him of his plan. Romeo did not know that his dear lady was only lying in the grave, waiting for the time when her husband would come to set her free from that cheerless place.

Just before he heard the news, Romeo had been unusually joyful and happy. He had dreamed in the night that he was dead, and that his lady came and found him dead and breathed such life with kisses into his lips that he lived again and was a king! Now that a messenger came from Verona, he thought it must be to tell him some good news of which his dream had been a sign. When he learned that it was the opposite of this, and that his wife was really dead and could not be brought back to life with any kisses, he ordered horses to be got ready so that he could visit Verona that night and see his lady in her grave.

As evil is quick to enter into the thoughts of hopeless men, he remembered a poor medicine-seller whose shop in Mantua he had recently passed. From the man's beggarly appearance, and the empty boxes standing on dirty shelves, he had said at the time, 'If a man needed poison, which by the law of Mantua it is death to sell, there is a poor creature here who would sell it to him.' He now went to find this man and told him what he wanted. The poor man put his doubts to one side when Romeo offered him some gold, and sold him a poison which he said would kill him quickly if he swallowed it, even if he had the strength of 20 men.

With this poison Romeo set out for Verona to see his dear

lady in her grave, intending then to take the poison and be buried by her side. He reached Verona at midnight and found the churchyard, in the middle of which stood the ancient grave of the Capulets. He had brought a light and some tools with him, and was just beginning to break open the door, when he was interrupted by a voice which called him by the name of "evil Montague" and ordered him to stop his unlawful business.

It was Paris, who had come to the grave of Juliet at this strange time of night to scatter flowers there, and to cry over the grave of the woman who should have been his wife. He did not know why Romeo was there, but, knowing that he was a Montague and therefore the enemy of all the Capulets, judged that he had come by night to do some shameful act to the dead bodies. So he angrily ordered him to stop, and called him a criminal, who, by the laws of Verona, had to be put to death if he were found within the walls of the city.

Romeo urged Paris to leave him, and warned him not to make him angry; he reminded Paris of the death of Tybalt, who lay buried there. But Paris would not listen to his warning and tried to take him as a criminal. Then they fought, and Paris fell.

Romeo had learnt on his way from Mantua that Paris should have married Juliet. So when he saw who it was that he had killed, he took the dead youth by the hand, as if misfortune had made a companion of him, and said that he would bury him in Juliet's grave.

He opened the grave, and there lay his lady, in perfect beauty, looking like one whom death had no power to change. She was as fresh as when she had fallen asleep; and near her lay Tybalt. When Romeo saw him, he begged pardon of his lifeless body, and, for Juliet, he called him "cousin" and said that he was about to put his enemy to death.

And now Romeo said his last goodbye to his lady, kissing her lips. Then he swallowed the poison which the medicine-seller had sold him. Its action was deadly and real, unlike that of the liquid which Juliet had drunk; the effect of her drug was now nearly at an end.

◆

The friar had by now learned that the letters which he had sent to Mantua had, by some unlucky chance, never reached Romeo. So he came himself, with tools and a light, to set the lady free from her early grave, because the hour had come at which he had promised that she would wake. But he was surprised to find a light already burning in the Capulets' grave, and to see swords and blood near it, and Romeo and Paris lying lifeless there.

Before he could try to imagine how these things had happened, Juliet woke out of her long sleep. Seeing the friar near her, she remembered where she was, and why she was there, and asked for Romeo.

Hearing a noise, the friar begged her to come out of that place of death and unnatural sleep, since a greater power than theirs had ruined all their plans. Then, frightened by the noise, he ran away.

When Juliet saw the cup in her true love's hand, she guessed that poison had been the cause of his death. She would have swallowed the remains if any had been left, and she kissed his lips to see if poison was still on them. Then, hearing a noise of people coming nearer, she quickly pulled out a knife which Romeo wore, struck herself with it, and died by his side.

The guards had arrived by this time. A servant of Paris, who had seen the fight between his master and Romeo, had gone to give warning of it. The news spread among the citizens, who went up and down the streets of Verona shouting in confusion. In the end the noise brought Lord Montague, Lord Capulet and the prince out of their beds to find out the cause of the noise. The friar had been caught by some of the guards as he was leaving the churchyard, trembling and crying in a suspicious manner. A great crowd had now collected at the Capulets' grave, and the friar was ordered by the prince to tell what he knew of these strange and terrible events.

There, in the presence of the old Lords Montague and Capulet, he told the story of their children's unfortunate love, and the part he had played in their marriage in the hope that such a union would end the long quarrels between their families. He said that Juliet, lying dead there, was Romeo's faithful wife, and Romeo, also dead there, was Juliet's husband. He told the prince that before he could find a suitable opportunity to make their marriage known, another marriage had been arranged for Juliet. To avoid it, Juliet had swallowed the sleeping medicine as he had advised, so that everyone thought that she was dead. Then he had written to Romeo, telling him to come and take her from the grave when the effect of the liquid was at an end, but unfortunately his letter had never reached Romeo. The friar could not continue the story further than this. He only knew that when he had come himself to free Juliet from that place of death, he had found both Romeo and Paris dead.

More of the story was supplied by the servant who had seen Paris and Romeo fight. The rest was told by the servant who had come with Romeo from Mantua, to whom this faithful lover had given letters for his father in the event of his death. These letters proved the truth of the friar's words. In them, Romeo admitted his marriage to Juliet and begged the forgiveness of his parents. He told them how he had bought poison and how he intended to come to the grave to die and lie with Juliet. All these facts saved the friar from any suspicion that he might have had a part in these killings.

Then the prince turned to these old lords, Montague and Capulet, and criticized them for their foolish quarrels. He showed them what a terrible punishment heaven had given them; it had found a way, even through the love of their children, to punish their unnatural hate.

These old families now agreed to bury their long quarrels in their children's graves. Lord Capulet asked Lord Montague to give him his hand, and called him by the name of brother as a sign that their families were now united. This hand, he said, was all he demanded. But Lord Montague said that he would give him more; he would put up a statue of Juliet in pure gold, which would be the richest and most perfect figure in all Verona. Lord Capulet, in return, said that he would put up a statue of Romeo.

So when it was too late, these poor old lords tried to do better than each other in their new-found friendship. But in the past, their anger and quarrels had been so violent that nothing but the terrible deaths of their children could remove the hates and jealousies of these two noble families.

Hamlet, Prince of Denmark

CHARACTERS
Claudius, King of Denmark
Hamlet, son of the last king, and nephew of the present one
Horatio, friend of Hamlet
Polonius, Minister of State
Laertes, son of Polonius
Marcellus, a guard
Ghost of Hamlet's father
A group of *Actors*
Gertrude, Queen of Denmark and mother of Hamlet
Ophelia, daughter of Polonius

Less than two months after the sudden death of King Hamlet, Gertrude, Queen of Denmark, married his brother Claudius. This was judged by everyone at that time to be a strangely unwise or unfeeling act, or even worse.

Claudius was in no way like her first husband in the qualities of his person or his mind. He was as worthless in appearance as he was evil in character. Some people even suspected that he had killed his brother, the last king, so that he could marry Gertrude and become King of Denmark himself. In this way he was able to prevent young Hamlet, the son of the buried king and his lawful heir, from becoming king.

This unwise action of the queen had a very great effect on the young prince, who loved and honoured the memory of his dead father. Being of a most honourable character himself, he was greatly troubled by the shame of his mother's marriage; shame, and grief at his father's death, made him fall into a state of deep sadness. He no longer found any pleasure in his books or his sports. He became tired of the world, which seemed to him like an uncared-for garden, in which all the best flowers have died for lack of space.

Although the loss of the crown was a bitter wound to this young prince, it was not this that troubled him and took away all his cheerful spirits – it was the fact that his mother had shown herself to be so forgetful of his father's memory. He had been so loving and so gentle a husband to her, and she had always appeared to be a loving wife to him. But in less than two months she had married his brother, young Hamlet's uncle. This in itself was a very improper and unlawful marriage, as they were such close relations, but it was made much worse by the speed with which it was done and by the unkingly character of the man whom she had chosen. It was this, much more than the loss of ten kingdoms, which made the young prince so unhappy.

Everything that his mother Gertrude or the king could do to try to raise his spirits was useless. He still appeared in court in black clothes, in memory of his father. He had not even taken it off on the day his mother was married, and he could not be persuaded to join in any of the celebrations on what seemed to him a shameful day.

He was most troubled by an uncertainty about the manner of his father's death. Claudius had made it known that a snake had bitten him. But young Hamlet had strong suspicions that Claudius himself was the snake, and that the snake that had bitten his father now wore his crown.

How right was this guess? What ought he to think of his mother? Had she known of this murder, and perhaps even agreed to it? These were the doubts which continued to worry him and were driving him mad.

◆

A story had reached the ear of young Hamlet that a ghost, exactly like the dead king, had been seen by the soldiers on guard in front of the palace at midnight. The figure was always dressed in the battledress which the dead king was known to have worn. Those who saw it (and Hamlet's close friend Horatio was one) agreed about the time and manner of its appearance. It came just as the clock struck midnight. It looked pale, with a face more of sorrow than of anger. Its beard was a dark silvery colour. It made no answer when they spoke to it. Once they thought it lifted up its head, and was about to speak; but at that moment morning broke, and it went quickly away and disappeared from their sight. Shocked at their story, the young prince believed that it was his father's ghost which they had seen. He decided to join the soldiers on guard that night so that he could have a chance of seeing it. He argued with himself that ghosts did not appear for no reason, but that this ghost must have something to tell. Although it had been silent until now, it would speak to him; and he waited with impatience for the coming of night.

When night came, he took his place with Horatio and Marcellus, one of the guards, in front of the palace where this spirit had been seen to walk. Their conversation was suddenly interrupted by Horatio, who said that the ghost was coming.

At the sight of his father's spirit, Hamlet was shocked and frightened. He called on heaven to protect them, since he did not know whether it was a good or bad spirit, whether it came for good or evil purposes. Gradually he became braver. His father (it seemed to him) looked at him so sadly, and appeared so exactly the same as when he was alive, that Hamlet could not help speaking to him. He called him by his name, 'Hamlet, King, Father!' and begged him to explain the reason why he had left his grave, where they had seen him quietly buried, to visit the earth and the moonlight again. Was there anything which they could do to give peace to his spirit?

The ghost made a sign to Hamlet, that he should go with him to some place further away where they could be alone. Horatio and Marcellus tried to stop the young prince from following the ghost, for they were afraid that it might be some evil spirit which would try to harm him. But their warnings and advice could not change Hamlet's mind. He cared too little about life to fear losing it; and as for his soul, he said, what could the spirit do to something that could never die?

When they were alone together, the spirit broke his silence, and told him that he was the ghost of Hamlet, his father, who had been cruelly murdered. He said that it had been done by his own brother Claudius, as Hamlet had already suspected, in the hope of winning his wife and his crown. As he was sleeping in his garden, which was always his custom in the afternoon, his faithless brother had stood over him, and poured into his ears a poisonous liquid that quickly killed him. So he was cut off by a brother's hand from his crown, his queen and his life. He begged Hamlet, if he had ever loved his dear father, to take revenge for this evil murder.

The ghost spoke sadly to his son about his mother's fall from goodness. She had proved so false to the memory of her first husband that she had married his murderer. But he told Hamlet that however he acted against his evil uncle, he must take care not to hurt his mother; he should leave her to heaven. Hamlet promised to obey the ghost's orders in all things, and the ghost disappeared.

When Hamlet was left alone, he promised himself that he would forget everything that he had ever learned. Nothing would live in his brain except the memory of what the ghost had told him and ordered him to do. He told the details of the conversation to no one except his dear friend Horatio, and he commanded both him and Marcellus to keep secret what they had seen that night.

◆

The terror which Hamlet had experienced at the sight of the ghost almost drove him mad. He feared that it would continue to have this effect, and that this might make his uncle suspicious, if the king suspected that Hamlet knew more of his father's death than he appeared to do. So from that time he decided to act as if he were really and truly mad. His dress, speech and behaviour became wild and strange, and he pretended to be a madman so excellently that the king and queen were both deceived. Not thinking that his grief for his father's death could produce such illness in his mind, they believed that it was caused by love.

Before Hamlet fell into this sad condition, he had dearly loved a beautiful girl called Ophelia, the daughter of Polonius, the king's chief minister. He had sent her letters and rings, and made many offers of love to her, and she had believed all his promises. But his unhappy state of mind made him forget her, and from the time when he pretended to be mad, he treated her with great unkindness.

She, good lady, did not want to blame him for being false to her, so she persuaded herself that it was only the illness in his mind which made him take less notice of her than before. She compared the qualities of his noble mind, now weakened by the deep sadness that troubled him, to sweet bells, which are able to give most beautiful music but which, when played out of tune, produce only a rough and unpleasant sound.

Although the business which Hamlet had in his mind – the punishment of his father's murderer – did not allow him to think of love, there were times when kind thoughts of Ophelia came to him. In one of these moments, when it seemed to him that his treatment of this gentle lady had been too cruel, he wrote her a letter full of wild words, which seemed to express his madness but were at the same time mixed with signs that he still cared.

These showed this honoured lady that a deep love for her still lay at the bottom of his heart. He told her to doubt that the stars were fire and to doubt that the sun moved, but never to doubt that he loved her.

Ophelia showed this letter to her father, and he felt it to be his duty to show it to the king and queen. From that moment they were sure that the true cause of Hamlet's madness was love. The queen certainly hoped that the beauty of Ophelia was the cause of his strangeness, and that her goodness would bring him back to his former way of life.

But Hamlet's illness lay deeper than she thought and it could not be cured by love. His father's ghost still filled his imagination, and the command to take revenge for his murder gave him no rest. Every hour of delay seemed to him to be wrong. But it was not easy to cause the death of the king, as he was always surrounded by his guards. Or if *they* were not there, Hamlet's mother was usually with her husband, and this stopped him from doing what he wanted to do. Also, the act of putting another creature to death was hateful and terrible to someone whose character was so naturally gentle as Hamlet's, and his sadness made him weak and anxious. Finally, he could not help having some doubts about whether the spirit he had seen was really his father, or whether it might have been the devil who had taken his father's shape in order to drive him to the act of murder. He decided that he would try to get more certain proof of the ghost's story, which might be false.

◆

While he was in this state of mind, some actors, who had often given Hamlet great pleasure in the past, came to the court. He had especially liked to hear one of them make a sad speech describing the death of old Priam, King of Troy, and the grief of Hecuba, his queen.

Hamlet welcomed his old friends and asked the actor if he would repeat that speech for him. He did so in a manner that almost made the scene come to life. He described the cruel murder of the weak old king, with the destruction of his people and city by fire; and he told of the mad grief of the old queen, running up and down the palace, with only a simple cloth on her head where a crown had been, and another to cover her body, where she had once worn a royal dress. The speech caused tears from everyone who stood near, and even the actor himself delivered it in a broken voice and with real tears in his eyes.

This made Hamlet realize that while that actor could put such great feeling into a story, and cry for Hecuba who had been dead for hundreds of years, he himself was so emotionless that he had let his revenge lie asleep all this time in dull forgetfulness.

While he was thinking about actors and acting, and the powerful effect which a good play has on those who see it, he remembered the case of a murderer who saw a murder on the stage and was so moved by the force of the scene that he admitted to the crime which he had done. He decided that these actors should play something like the murder of his father in front of his uncle, and he would watch closely to see what effect it might have on the king; he could then make up his mind with more certainty if he were the murderer or not. He ordered a play to be prepared, and invited the king and queen to attend its performance.

The story of the play was the murder of a duke in Vienna. The duke's name was Gonzago, and his wife's was Baptista. The play showed how a certain Lucianus, a near relation of the duke, poisoned him in his garden to get his property, and how the murderer soon afterwards won the love of Gonzago's wife.

At the performance of this play, the king, who did not know the trap which was set for him, was present with his queen and the whole court. Hamlet sat very near him to watch his expressions. The play began with a conversation between Gonzago and his wife. In this the lady made many promises of love and said that she would never marry a second husband if she lived longer than Gonzago. She even wished that God would strike her down if she ever took a second husband, and added that no women did so except those who kill their first husbands.

Hamlet saw the king change colour at these words, and knew that it was hateful both to him and to the queen. But when Lucianus, according to the story, came to poison Gonzago while he was asleep in his garden, Claudius was so nervous that he was unable to sit through the rest of the play. Calling for lights, and pretending or feeling a sudden sickness, he quickly left the theatre. After he had gone, the play was stopped.

Now Hamlet had seen enough to be satisfied that the words of the ghost were true. He swore to Horatio that he would believe everything it had said. But before he could make up his mind what form his revenge should take, now that he knew his uncle to be his father's murderer, his mother asked him to attend a private meeting in her room.

◆

It was the king's wish that the queen should send for Hamlet, so that she could inform her son how much his recent behaviour had displeased them both. Wishing to know all that happened at this meeting, and thinking that Hamlet's mother might not tell him everything that Hamlet said, the king ordered old Polonius to hide behind the curtains in the queen's room; there, unseen, he could hear all their conversation.

As soon as Hamlet came, his mother began to speak angrily about his bad behaviour. She told him that he had given great offence to *his* father – she meant the king, his uncle, to whom she was now married.

Hamlet was angry that she should give such a dear and

respectful name as father to the murderer of his true father, and he replied, sharply, 'Mother, *you* have much offended *my* father.'

The queen asked him if he had forgotten who he was speaking to.

'Oh!' replied Hamlet. 'I wish I could forget. You are the queen, your husband's brother's wife; and you are my mother. I wish you were not what you are.' Taking her by the wrist, made her sit down. He wanted to try to make her understand everything that was wrong with the way she was living.

She was frightened by his strange manner and worried that, in his madness, he might harm her. She cried out, and a voice was heard from behind the curtains, 'Help, help, the queen!'

When Hamlet heard this, he thought it was the king himself who was hidden there. He pulled out his sword and struck at the place where the voice came from. At last the voice stopped and he believed the person to be dead. When he pulled out the body, though, he found that it was not the king – it was Polonius, the old minister, who had hidden there as a secret listener.

'Oh!' shouted the queen. 'What a foolish and bloody act!'

'A bloody act, mother,' replied Hamlet, 'but not as bad as yours, when you killed a king and married his brother.'

Hamlet had said too much to stop here. Even though the faults of parents should be treated gently by their children, in the case of great crimes a son may speak with some unkindness to his own mother, as long as that unkindness is meant for her good and to turn her from her bad ways. This good prince, in moving words, showed the queen that she was wrong to be so forgetful of the dead king, his father; he reminded her that in a short space of time she married his brother, his suspected murderer. After the promises which she had made to her first husband, such an act was enough to make people doubt all promises made by women, to think that all goodness was a pretence, and their religion only a form of words.

He showed her two pictures — one of the late king, her first husband, and the other of the present king, her second husband — and he told her to notice the difference. What nobility there was on his father's face! How like a god he looked! And how ugly the second face was, the face of a man who had destroyed his own good brother. And the queen was bitterly ashamed that he was forcing her to look at her own soul, which she now saw was so black and evil.

Then Hamlet asked her how she could continue to live with Claudius and be a wife to the man who had murdered her first husband, and stolen his crown . . .

As he was speaking, the ghost of his father entered the room. In great fear, Hamlet asked what it wanted. The ghost said that it had come to remind him of the revenge which Hamlet had promised but seemed to have forgotten. It also told him to speak to his mother again before her grief and fear killed her. Then it disappeared, and was seen only by Hamlet. He could not make his mother see it either by pointing to where it stood or by any description of it. But she was greatly frightened all this time to hear him talking to nothing, as it seemed to her; and she believed it to be the result of the disorder in his mind.

Hamlet begged her not to think that it was his madness, rather than her own offences, which had brought his father's spirit to earth again. He told her to feel the beating of his heart — how regular it was, not like a madman's. And he begged her, with tears in his eyes, to admit to heaven what was past, and in future to avoid the company of the king. When she showed herself to be a mother to him by respecting his father's memory, he would ask her to forgive him as a son. She promised to do what he asked.

Now Hamlet had time to consider who it was that he had unfortunately and unwisely killed. When he saw that it was Polonius, the father of Ophelia, whom he so dearly loved, he cried bitterly for what he had done.

The death of Polonius gave the king an excuse to send Hamlet out of the kingdom. He would gladly have put him to death, but he feared the people, who liked Hamlet, and the queen, who, in spite of all her faults, loved her son dearly. Pretending to provide for Hamlet's safety, so that he would not be punished for Polonius's death, Claudius put him on a ship to England in the care of two men from his court. He sent letters with these men to the English court (which at that time was ruled by Denmark), giving orders that Hamlet should be put to death as soon as he landed on English ground.

Hamlet suspected some dishonesty, and found the letters secretly at night. He rubbed out his own name and put in its place the names of the two men who were in charge of him, so that they would be put to death. Then, closing the letters, he put them back where he had found them.

Soon after this, the ship was attacked and a fight started. During this fight, Hamlet showed his courage by jumping, with his sword in his hand, on to the enemy's ship. His own ship sailed away in fear, leaving him to his death. The two men from the king's court went on to England, carrying the letters which Hamlet had changed.

But the attackers proved to be gentle enemies. Knowing that their prisoner was the prince, and hoping that he would speak for them at court, they put Hamlet on shore at the nearest port in Denmark. From this place, he wrote to the king, telling him of the strange chance which had brought him back to his own country, and saying that he would return to the court the next day. When he arrived home, the first thing that met his eyes was a very sad sight.

This was the funeral of the young and beautiful Ophelia, once his dear lady. From the time of her father's death, this young girl had begun to lose her mind. She suffered so much because he had been cruelly killed by the prince whom she loved, that in a short time she became quite mad.

There was a beautiful tree which grew over a stream, and you could see its leaves in the water. She came here one day, with crowns of leaves and grass which she had made. She was climbing up to hang these in the tree when a branch broke, and she was thrown into the water. Her clothes held her up for a time, but it was not long before her clothes, heavy with water, pulled her down to a muddy and miserable death.

It was this beautiful lady's funeral, attended by her brother Laertes, the king, the queen and the whole court, which was being performed when Hamlet arrived. He did not know what all this ceremony meant at first, and stood on one side. He saw the flowers scattered on the grave, which the queen herself threw in; and as she did so, she said, 'I ought to have scattered them on your marriage bed, sweet girl, not on your grave. You should have been my Hamlet's wife.'

He saw Laertes jump into the grave, mad with grief, and tell the gravediggers to pile mountains of earth on him so that he might be buried with her.

Then Hamlet's love for this beautiful girl came back to him, and he could not bear that a brother should show such grief, when he loved Ophelia better than forty thousand brothers. He came out from where he stood and jumped into the grave where Laertes was, even madder than he. Laertes thought of Hamlet as the cause of his father's and his sister's death, and seized him by the throat as an enemy, until they were separated.

After the funeral, Hamlet begged forgiveness for having thrown himself into the grave. He said that he could not bear that anyone should show more grief than himself at the death of the beautiful Ophelia. And for a time these two noble young men seemed to be friends again.

The king, Hamlet's evil uncle, planned to use Laertes's grief and anger over the death of his father and Ophelia to destroy Hamlet. He persuaded Laertes to call on Hamlet to see which of them was more skilful in a friendly sword fight. Hamlet accepted, and a day was fixed for the match.

The whole court was present at this match, and Laertes, by order of the king, prepared a poisoned weapon. Hamlet chose a sword; he did not suspect Laertes of being disloyal, so he did not examine Laertes's weapon carefully. Instead of a sword without a point, which the laws demanded, Laertes used one with a point, and poisoned.

At first Laertes only played with Hamlet, and allowed him to gain some advantage. The king pretended to be pleased with this, and praised Hamlet's success. But soon Laertes became angry, cut Hamlet with his poisoned weapon, and gave him his death wound. Hamlet still did not know the truth, but he became more violent too and, in the struggle, exchanged his own weapon for Laertes's poisoned one. With this he repaid Laertes for the stroke he had given him, so that Laertes was caught by his own dishonesty.

At this moment the queen cried out that she had been poisoned. She had accidentally drunk out of a bowl which the king had prepared for Hamlet, in case he got warm in the fight and called for a drink. Into this the evil king had put a deadly poison, to make sure of Hamlet's death if Laertes failed. He had forgotten to warn the queen about this bowl, and she died immediately.

Hamlet now suspected some evil, and ordered the doors to be shut while he tried to discover it. Feeling his life leaving him as a result of the wound which Hamlet had given him, Laertes told Hamlet about the poisoned point, and said that Hamlet had less than an hour to live, as no medicine could cure him. With his last words, he accused the king of being the one who had planned these evil acts. Then, begging Hamlet's forgiveness, he died.

When Hamlet understood that his end was near, he suddenly turned on his false uncle and pushed the point of the poisoned sword into his heart. With this action he completed the promise which he had made to his father's spirit that he would take revenge for his murder.

Then, feeling that his breath was failing, Hamlet turned to his dear friend Horatio, who had watched all these sad events. It seemed for a moment as if Horatio would kill himself to go to his death with the prince, but Hamlet begged him to live so that he could tell his story to the world. Horatio promised that he would make a true report, since he knew of everything that had happened.

Satisfied, the noble heart of Hamlet stopped beating; and Horatio, with many tears, prayed for the spirit of this sweet prince. Hamlet was a loving and gentle prince, and greatly admired for his many noble and princely qualities. If he had lived, he would no doubt have proved a most royal and excellent King of Denmark.

Othello

CHARACTERS
Brabantio, a senator
Othello, a noble Moor★ in the service of the state of Venice
Cassio, his lieutenant
Iago, an officer
Montano, another officer
Desdemona, daughter of Brabantio, and wife of Othello
Emilia, wife of Iago

Brabantio, a rich senator of Venice, had a beautiful daughter, the gentle Desdemona. Many men wanted to marry her, both for her many good qualities and for her rich expectations. But she saw no one that she really desired among the lovers of her own country and colour, and she had chosen as the object of her love a Moor, a black man, whom her father liked and often invited to his house. This man, Othello, seemed to have everything that might make him attractive, even to the greatest lady. He was a soldier, and a brave one. By his actions in bloody wars against the Turks, he had risen to the rank of general in the Venetian service, and he was respected and trusted by the state.

He had been a traveller, and Desdemona loved to hear him tell the story of his adventures. He described the battles in which he had fought; the dangers he had met by land and sea; his narrow escapes; how he had been taken prisoner by the enemy, and sold into slavery; and how he had escaped. Then he told of

★Moor: a Muslim person of the Arab race which was in power from 711 to 1492.

the strange things he had seen in foreign countries: the great deserts, the plains, the rocks and mountains whose heads were in the clouds; of wild people who were man-eaters, and a race of men in Africa whose heads grew beneath their shoulders.

These travellers' stories held Desdemona's attention so much that if she were called away at any time, she would quickly finish her business and return with eagerness to listen to more of them. Once she begged him to tell her the whole story of his life, of which she had heard so much but only in parts. He agreed to do so, and made her cry many a tear when he spoke of some terrible blow which he had suffered in his youth.

When his story was finished, she swore prettily that it was all most strange, and moving and pitiful. She wished (she said) she had not heard it, but she also wished that heaven had made her such a man. Then she thanked him, and told him that if he had a friend who loved her, he only had to teach him how to tell his story and that would win her. When she said this, honestly but quietly, Othello understood what she meant, spoke more openly of his love for her, and so gained the agreement of the generous Lady Desdemona to marry him.

Neither Othello's colour nor his fortune made him acceptable to Brabantio as his daughter's husband. He had expected that before long she would choose a husband of the rank of senator, as most noble Venetian ladies did. In this, though, he was deceived. Desdemona loved Othello, and gave her heart to his brave qualities. His colour, which to all other ladies would have been a strong objection, was valued by her above all the white skins and clear faces of the young Venetian nobles who wished to marry her.

Their marriage was privately performed, but could not be kept a secret for long. When it came to the ears of the old man, Brabantio, he charged Othello before the council of the senate with having gained the love of Desdemona by magic and caused her to marry him without her father's permission.

At this time the state of Venice had urgent need of Othello's services. News had arrived that a great many Turkish ships were on their way to the island of Cyprus, intending to take that place back from the Venetians, who were holding it at that time. It was thought that Othello was the most suitable man to defend Cyprus against the Turks. So Othello now stood in the presence of the senators, both as one who was needed for a great state employment, and as a criminal charged with offences that were punishable by death.

The senators listened patiently to Brabantio, because of his age and character. But he made so many wild and foolish charges that when Othello was called on to defend himself, he only needed to tell them the story of his love. He told them exactly how he had won the love of Desdemona, and delivered his speech with such noble honesty that the chief judge could not help admitting that a story told in such a way would have won *his* daughter too. It soon appeared quite plain that Othello had, in his lovemaking, used only the honest arts of men in love; the only magic he had employed had been his ability to tell a soft story to win a lady's ear.

This statement by Othello was proved to be true by the words of the Lady Desdemona herself. She appeared in court and, while openly admitting that she owed her life and education to her father, begged him to allow her to admit an even higher debt to her lord and husband.

Unable to prove his case, the old senator called the Moor to him with many expressions of sorrow, and gave his daughter to him. If he had been free to keep her back (he told him), he would have done so with all his heart. He added that he was glad that he had no other child, for this behaviour of Desdemona would have taught him to be cruel.

Now that this difficulty had been overcome, Othello quickly promised to manage the wars in Cyprus, and Desdemona cheerfully agreed that he could go if she was allowed to go with him.

◆

As soon as Othello and his lady landed in Cyprus, news arrived that a storm had scattered the Turkish ships, and so the island was safe from any fear of an immediate attack. But the war which Othello himself was about to suffer was now beginning, and the enemies, with their evil tongues, who encouraged him to hate his guiltless lady would prove more terrible than any Turk.

Among all the general's friends, no one possessed Othello's trust more completely than Cassio. Michael Cassio was a young soldier from Florence. He was bright, good-looking and well spoken, favourite qualities with women. He was exactly the sort of person that might excite the jealousy of an older man (like Othello) who had married a young and beautiful wife; but Othello was as free from jealousy as he was noble, and as unable to suspect an evil action as he was to do one.

He had employed Cassio as a kind of messenger in his love affair with Desdemona, because he feared that he did not have the soft tongue which pleases ladies and was found in his friend. It is not surprising, then, that the gentle Desdemona loved and trusted Cassio next to Othello himself.

The marriage of this pair had not made any difference in their behaviour to Michael Cassio. He often visited their house, and his free and amusing talk was a pleasant change to Othello, who was more serious. Desdemona and Cassio talked and laughed together, as they had in the days when he had gone lovemaking instead of his friend.

Othello had recently raised Cassio to a higher rank, a position of trust just below the general himself. This had given great offence to Iago, an older officer who thought he had a better claim than Cassio. He often made fun of Cassio as a man fit only for the company of ladies, and one who did not know any more than a girl about the art of war or how to prepare an army for battle.

Iago hated Cassio. He also hated Othello, not only for preferring Cassio but also because he had a suspicion that he was too fond of Iago's own wife Emilia, Desdemona's servant. Angered by these things, Iago's evil mind thought of a terrible plan for revenge which would cause the ruin of Cassio, Othello and Desdemona as well.

Iago had studied human nature closely. He knew that, of all the pains which trouble the mind of man (and much greater than bodily pain), those of jealousy were the most unbearable and had the sorest sting. If he could succeed in making Othello jealous of Cassio, he thought it would be a perfect revenge and might end in the death of Cassio or Othello or both.

◆

The arrival of the general and his lady in Cyprus, together with the news of the scattering of the enemy's ships, caused celebrations on the island. Everybody had fun. Wine flowed plentifully, and the healths of Othello and the beautiful Desdemona were drunk.

Cassio was in charge of the guard that night. He had orders from Othello to keep the soldiers from drinking too much, so that there were no noisy disorders to make people fear the newly landed army.

That night Iago began to put his plans in action. Pretending loyalty and love for the general, he persuaded Cassio to have a lot to drink (a great fault in an officer who is on guard). For a time Cassio refused, but soon he was swallowing glass after glass of wine. Then his tongue began to praise Desdemona, whose health he drank again and again, saying that she was a most beautiful lady; until, in the end, he lost all good sense.

Iago now encouraged another man to quarrel with Cassio, and they pulled out their swords. When Montano, an honourable officer, tried to stop the fight, he himself was wounded. The noise and disorder now began to spread, and Iago, who had begun it all, was the first to give warning of it. He caused the castle bell to be rung, as if some dangerous rising of men against their officers had begun instead of a slight drunken quarrel. The ringing of the bell woke Othello. He dressed in a hurry and, arriving at the scene of action, questioned Cassio about the cause of the problem.

Cassio had now returned to his senses as the effect of the wine had begun to disappear, but he was too ashamed to reply. Iago pretended that he did not want to blame Cassio, but was forced to do so by Othello, who demanded to know the truth; he gave an account of the whole matter (leaving out his own part in it, which Cassio was unable to remember because of the amount he had drunk) in such a way that he made Cassio's offence appear greater than it was. The result was that Othello, a firm believer in order, was forced to take away from Cassio the position to which he had raised him. So Iago's first trick succeeded completely. He had now weakened his hated enemy and made him lose his rank.

Cassio now said sadly to Iago, who still seemed to be his friend, that he had been a fool to drink so much. He was ruined, because he could not ask the general for his position again. He hated himself.

Iago said that he, or any man living, might drink too much occasionally. Now they must try to repair the damage which had been done. The general's wife was now the general, and could do anything with Othello. Cassio must beg Desdemona to make peace for him with her lord. Her kindness would make her agree to a good service of this sort; Cassio would become the general's friend again, and this crack in their love would soon disappear. This would have been good advice from Iago if it had not been given for evil purposes.

Cassio did as Iago advised him, and went to the Lady Desdemona, who was easily persuaded to do what he asked. She promised Cassio that she would beg her lord to forgive him, and would rather die than give up his case.

She immediately began to do so in such a serious and pretty manner that Othello could not stop her. Othello was very angry with Cassio. When he said that it was too soon to forgive such an offender, though, his wife refused to be discouraged, but demanded that it should be the next night, or the morning after, or the morning after that at the latest. Then she showed how sorry poor Cassio was, and said that his offence did not deserve so great a punishment.

When Othello still would not agree, she said, 'What, my lord! Do I really have to beg for Cassio, Michael Cassio, who came lovemaking for you, and often took your side when I said something against you! I think this is a little thing to ask of you. When I mean to test your love, I shall ask for something much greater.' Othello could refuse nothing to such prayers, and he promised to look kindly on Michael Cassio again, but in his own time.

It happened that Othello and Iago had entered the room where Desdemona was just as Cassio, who had been begging her to help him, was leaving by the opposite door. Iago said in a low voice, as if to himself, 'I do not like that.'

Othello did not take much notice of what he said. The meeting which then took place with his lady put it out of his head; but he remembered it afterwards. When Desdemona had gone, Iago asked Othello whether, when Othello was trying to win his lady for his wife, Michael Cassio knew of his love.

The general said that he did, and added that he had often acted as messenger between them. Iago looked thoughtful, as if he now understood more about some terrible matter, and cried, 'Really!'

This brought into Othello's mind the words which Iago had spoken on entering the room, when he had seen Cassio with Desdemona. He began to think there was some meaning in all this, since he considered Iago to be a fair and honest man. What would be tricks in a false creature seemed, in Iago, to be the natural working of a loyal mind. So Othello begged Iago to tell what he knew and put his worst thoughts into words.

'And what,' said Iago, 'if some evil thoughts should have found entrance into my heart?'

Then Iago went on to say that it would be a pity if any trouble should come to Othello as a result of his lack of attention; that it would not help Othello's peace of mind to know his thoughts; and that people's good names must not be taken away for slight suspicions. When Othello's interest was raised almost to madness by these suggestions, Iago begged him to guard against jealousy. This evil man raised suspicions in Othello very cleverly by warning him to take no notice of such doubts.

'I know,' said Othello, 'that my wife is beautiful; loves company and good times; is free in speech; sings, plays and dances well: but where goodness is, these qualities are good. I must have proof before I can think that she is unfaithful.'

As if he were glad that Othello was slow to believe that his lady had done anything wrong, Iago openly declared that he had no proof. But he begged Othello to watch her behaviour carefully when Cassio was near. He must not be jealous, but he must not feel too confident either, because he (Iago) knew the characters of Italian ladies better than Othello could do. In Venice, he said, the wives let heaven see many tricks that they dared not show their husbands. He cleverly suggested that Desdemona had deceived her father when she married Othello, and had kept it such a secret that the poor old man thought magic had been used. Othello was much moved by this argument; if she had deceived her father, why might she not deceive her husband?

Iago begged his pardon for having worried him; but Othello – pretending not to care, while he was really shaken with grief at Iago's words – asked him to continue. Iago appeared not to want to, as if he had no wish to prove anything against Cassio, whom he called his friend.

He reminded Othello that Desdemona had refused many suitable husbands of her own country and colour, and had married him, a Moor. This showed her to be unnatural and to have a determined will. When her better judgement returned, it was probable that she would begin to compare Othello with the fine figures and clear white faces of young Italians. He ended by advising Othello to delay his forgiveness of Cassio a little longer, and to note how eagerly Desdemona asked for that forgiveness.

In this evil way, this clever deceiver planned to use the gentle qualities of this lady to destroy her, and to trap her with a net of her own goodness. First he had encouraged Cassio to beg Desdemona to help him, and then he planned to use that to ruin her.

The meeting ended when Iago begged Othello to believe that there was no guilt in his wife until he had more certain proof; and Othello promised to be patient.

◆

But from that moment Othello was never happy. Nothing could ever bring back that sweet rest which he had enjoyed only yesterday. He grew tired of his job. He no longer took pleasure in the profession of arms. His heart, which used to jump with excitement at the sight of soldiers ready for battle or the sound of a drum, seemed to have lost all pride and purpose. His eagerness and all his old joys disappeared.

Sometimes he thought that his wife was honest, and at times

he thought that she was not. Sometimes he thought that Iago was right, and at times he thought that he was wrong. Then he wished that he had never found out. If she loved Cassio, it made no difference to him, as long as he did not know. Torn to pieces by such thoughts as these, he seized Iago's throat on one occasion and demanded proof of Desdemona's guilt; he threatened him with death for lying about her if there *was* no proof.

Pretending to be angry because his honesty was being doubted, Iago asked Othello if he had not sometimes seen a handkerchief spotted with berries in his wife's hand.

Othello answered that he had given it to her, and that it was his first gift.

'I saw Michael Cassio today with that same handkerchief,' said Iago.

'If you are telling the truth,' said Othello, 'I will not rest until my revenge has swallowed them up. First, to prove your loyalty, I expect Cassio to be put to death within three days. As for that beautiful devil, my wife, I will go away and think of a quick means of death for her.'

To a jealous man, small and unimportant things are strong proofs. A handkerchief of his wife's seen in Cassio's hand was reason enough for the deceived Othello to send them both to their death, without even asking how Cassio had obtained it. Desdemona had never given such a present to Cassio, and she would never have thought of doing so. Neither Cassio nor Desdemona were guilty of any offence against Othello. The evil Iago had made his wife (a good but weak woman) steal this handkerchief from Desdemona, pretending that she wanted to have a copy made. But Iago's real purpose was to leave it where Cassio might find it, and so give support to his suggestion that it was a present from Desdemona.

Meeting his wife soon afterwards, Othello pretended that he had a headache, and asked her to lend him her handkerchief to hold to his head to ease it.

She did so.

'Not this,' said Othello. 'but that handkerchief I gave you.'

Desdemona had not got it with her (since it had been stolen, as we have said).

'What have you done!' said Othello. 'An Egyptian woman gave that handkerchief to my mother. She told her that while she kept it, my father would love her. If she lost it, or gave it away, my father's love would change and he would hate her as much as he had loved her. When she was dying, she gave it to me. She told me to give it to my wife if I ever married.'

'Is it possible?' said the frightened lady.

'It is true,' continued Othello, 'it is a magic handkerchief.'

Desdemona was ready to die with fear. She knew that she had lost it, and she feared that with it she had lost her husband's love.

Othello continued to demand the handkerchief. When she could not produce it, she tried to turn her husband away from such serious thoughts. She cheerfully suggested that all his talk about the handkerchief was meant to prevent her from speaking for Michael Cassio, whom she began to praise (as Iago had said she would). Othello hurried out of the room in anger, and then Desdemona began to suspect that her lord was jealous.

She could not think what cause she had given him for this, so then she blamed herself for thinking so badly of the noble Othello. She thought that perhaps some unpleasant news from Venice or some state troubles had made him angry.

'Men are not gods,' she told herself. 'We must not expect such gentleness from them when they are married as they show us on the wedding day.' Then she was angry with herself again for judging his unkindness so unkindly.

When Othello and Desdemona met again, he charged her more clearly with being unfaithful, and with loving another man whom he did not name. He told her that he could have suffered all sorts of evils bravely – illness, shame, lack of money – but her unfaithfulness had broken his heart. While he swore at her, he also said that she looked so beautiful and smelt so sweet; and he wished she had never been born.

◆

When he had left her, this poor lady was so filled with confusion at her lord's false suspicion of her that she felt ready to fall into a deep sleep and told her servant to prepare her bed. When people teach their babies, she thought, they do it by gentle means – and Othello could have blamed her in this way. This was her only complaint.

Desdemona went to bed expecting her lord to follow her. As soon as she had fallen into a troubled sleep, though, Othello entered the room intending to put his lady to death. When he saw her asleep, he thought he would not make her bleed or mark that beautiful white skin of hers. But he was determined that she should die. If not (as he said), she would live to be unfaithful to more men, as she had been to him. Then he kissed her for the last time, but that kiss was so sweet that he was forced to kiss her again.

Desdemona was woken by his kisses. She looked at Othello, saw him bite his bottom lip and roll his eyes, and knew that he was always to be feared when he looked like this. He told her to prepare for death, and to say her prayers, since he would not kill her soul.

This guiltless wife begged for pity, and asked to know her fault. Then he named Cassio, and the handkerchief which (he said) she had given him. Just as the lady was beginning to explain, he suddenly refused to hear any more; covering her with the bedclothes, he stopped her breathing until she died.

◆

At the same moment, Cassio was brought wounded and bleeding into the house. Iago had sent one of his men to murder him, but he had not succeeded, and the man had been killed by Iago to prevent discovery of his plan. Some letters were found in this man's pockets which made Iago's guilt, and Cassio's honour, perfectly clear. Cassio now came to beg Othello's pardon, and to ask in what way he had offended him to make him employ Iago to murder him.

This discovery was a great shock to Othello. He now understood that he was no better than a murderer himself, and that his wife had always been faithful to him. The pain and sorrow which this discovery gave him made life unbearable. He fell on his sword and, throwing himself on the body of his dear dead lady, died too.

These terrible acts shocked and frightened those who were present. Othello had always had a good name and until he was deceived by the evil ways of a disloyal man, he had been a most loving husband. He had loved – not wisely, but too well; and when he was dead all his former goodness and his brave actions were remembered.

Only two things remained to be done. Iago was sent to a painful death; and the state and people of Venice were told of the sad end of their famous general.

ACTIVITIES

Introduction

1 Check the meanings of these words in your dictionary.
   comedy   tale
   a Which word is a type of play?
   b Which word is a type of story?
   c Give some examples of *comedies* you have seen or read.

The Winter's Tale

Before you read

2 This is the story of a jealous husband. What effects can jealousy have, in your experience? Can it ever be a positive emotion?
3 Find these words in your dictionary. They are all in the story.
   *feast   oracle   heir   shepherd   kingdom   statue
   misery   noble*
   Complete the crossword using the new words.

Clues across

   1 a country governed by a king or queen
   4 someone whose job is to look after sheep
   6 someone who could give people advice from the gods
   7 a large meal to celebrate a special occasion

Clues down

1 morally good and generous
3 great unhappiness
4 a figure made of stone
5 a person who will receive someone's property when they die

After you read

4 Describe the relationships between:
  a Leontes and Polixenes
  b Hermione and Perdita
  c Perdita and Leontes
5 Explain how Leontes loses his love for the queen and then finds it again.

King Lear

Before you read

6 Lear, an old man, gives away his kingdom to two of his three daughters. What do you think the advantages and disadvantages of this arrangement will be for him?
7 Check the meanings of these words in your dictionary:
  crown duke earl
  a Which words refer to people?
  b Which word is something royal?

After you read

8 Who:
  a really loves her father?
  b is sent out of Britain in spite of his loyalty?
  c becomes Queen of France?
  d does King Lear visit first?
  e are Lear's true friends?
  f falls on his knees in front of his daughter?
  g poisons Regan?
  h kills herself?
  i is killed in prison?
  j dies of grief?

9 Act out the first meeting between Lear and Cordelia after her return from France.

10 Discuss what you think a child's duties to his or her father should be.

The Taming of the Shrew

Before you read

11 Find these words in your dictionary:

shrew   tame

  a A shrew is a kind of small animal, but the word also has another meaning. Find it and translate the title of the play into your own language.

  b What other animals are used to describe people in your language?

After you read

12 Explain why:

  a Baptista is worried about his oldest daughter.

  b Petruchio wants to marry Katharine.

  c Petruchio behaves so badly at the wedding.

  d Petruchio makes his wife beg for food.

  e Katharine says, of the sun, 'Whatever you wish to call it, that is what it is . . .'.

  f Petruchio makes a bet with two other men.

13 Discuss the best adjectives to describe these people:

  a Katharine, at the beginning of the story

  b Katharine, at the end of the story

  c Petruchio

Romeo and Juliet

Before you read

14 What do you know about the story of Romeo and Juliet?

15 Use your dictionary to find the meanings of these words:

angel   friar   mask

Match the words to the correct meanings.

a something that covers your face

b a spirit who lives with God In heaven

c a religious man

16 What do these people feel for each other?

a Romeo and Rosaline

b Romeo and Juliet

c Tybalt and Romeo

17 Which of these people are dead by the end of the story?
How do they die?

a Romeo

b Juliet

c Tybalt

d Benvolio

e Mercutio

f Friar Lawrence

g Paris

h The Prince of Verona

18 Describe the part that these people play in the story:

a the friar

b the Prince of Verona

Hamlet, Prince of Denmark

Before you read

19 Look at the list of characters and complete these sentences.

a The ghost is the spirit of Claudius's ....

b Claudius is Hamlet's ....

c Gertrude is Claudius's ....

d The ghost is the spirit of Gertrude's ....

20 What causes these people to be so unhappy?

   a Hamlet

   b the ghost of Hamlet's father

   c Ophelia

21 How far do you agree with this view of Hamlet's character?

   'Hamlet was a loving and gentle prince, and greatly admired for his
many noble and princely qualities.'

   How would *you* describe him?

Othello

Before you read

22 Othello says of his wife, 'I must have proof before I can think that
she is unfaithful.' What kind of proof might he look for?

23 Find these words in your dictionary:

   lieutenant   senator

   Group the words below with one of the above words.

government	*officer*
elect	*politician*
army	*soldier*

After you read

24 Answer these questions.

   a Why does Brabantio object to Othello's marriage to his daughter?

   b Why does Desdemona marry Othello?

   c Why does Iago hate Othello?

   d What 'proof' is Othello given of his wife's guilt?

   e How does Desdemona die?

   f How does Othello die?

   g What happens to Iago?

25 Explain the part that Cassio plays in the story.

26 Discuss how Iago manages to turn Othello against his wife.

Writing

27 Explain the importance of jealousy in one of these stories.

28 Tell the story of one of the plays from the point of view of a less important character.

29 Compare the stories of *The Winter's Tale* and *Othello*. Explain why one is described as a comedy and the other a tragedy.

30 What part does revenge play in these stories?

31 Describe the way that the children in the stories behave towards their parents. Do you recognize these forms of behaviour among people you know?

32 Which character do you feel most sympathy for? Explain why.

Answers for the Activities in this book are published in our free resource packs for teachers, the Penguin Readers Factsheets, or available on a separate sheet. Please write to your local Pearson Education office or to: Marketing Department, Penguin Longman Publishing, 5 Bentinck Street, London W1M 5RN.